George Henry Gerberding

New Testament conversions

A series of sermons

George Henry Gerberding

New Testament conversions
A series of sermons

ISBN/EAN: 9783337264734

Printed in Europe, USA, Canada, Australia, Japan

Cover: Foto ©Lupo / pixelio.de

More available books at **www.hansebooks.com**

New Testament Conversions:

A SERIES OF SERMONS

BY

REV. G. H. GERBERDING, A. M.,

PASTOR OF ST. MARK'S ENGLISH EVANGELICAL LUTHERAN CHURCH, FARGO, DAKOTA, AUTHOR OF "THE WAY OF SALVATION IN THE LUTHERAN CHURCH."

PUBLISHED FOR THE AUTHOR.

SECOND THOUSAND.

LUTHERAN PUBLICATION SOCIETY,
PHILADELPHIA, PA.

TO

THE CAUSE OF A HEARTY, HEALTHY,
LIVING PIETY,
WHICH SPRINGS NOT FROM SUPERFICIAL SENTIMENTALISM, OR
OCCASIONAL EMOTIONALISM; A PIETY THAT GROWS OUT
OF A CORRECT UNDERSTANDING, A TRUE APPRE-
CIATION AND A PRAYERFUL, DILIGENT USE
OF THE CHRIST-ORDAINED MEANS OF
GRACE, THIS BOOK IS DEDICATED
BY

THE AUTHOR.

CONTENTS.

	PAGE
INTRODUCTION	9

SERMON I.

CONVERSION: ITS NATURE, NECESSITY AND EFFICIENT AGENCIES 15

SERMON II.

THE WOMAN OF SAMARIA 31

SERMON III.

THE PRODIGAL SON 43

CONTENTS.

PAGE

SERMON IV.
THE PUBLICAN 57

SERMON V.
ZACCHEUS 71

SERMON VI.
PETER, FALL AND RE-CONVERSION OF 85

SERMON VII.
THE DYING THIEF 101

SERMON VIII.
TESTS AND FRUITS OF PETER'S RE-CONVERSION 117

SERMON IX.
THE THREE THOUSAND 133

SERMON X.

THE ETHIOPIAN EUNUCH 151

SERMON XI.

PAUL'S CONVERSION 167

SERMON XII.

CORNELIUS 185

SERMON XIII.

SERGIUS PAULUS 201

SERMON XIV.

LYDIA 215

SERMON XV.

THE JAILER 233

SERMON XVI.

A Spurious Conversion 251

SERMON XVII.

Almost Converted 263

INTRODUCTION.

"Of the making of books, there is no end." If this was true in Solomon's day, how much more true in our day?

The saying of the wise man can also be applied to many special departments of literature. It can be said with truth, "of the making of *sermon* books, there is no end." Why, then, send forth another Book of Sermons?

Does it bring out truths unknown before? Does it occupy ground unused before? Does it treat of subjects not handled in the past? No! It sets forth truth as old as Revelation. It tills in fields that have been broken and dragged and rolled by all sorts of ploughmen and teams and implements. It treats of a trite and worn and common subject.

God was treating of it and aiming at it when He said in Eden: "*Adam, where art thou?*" God's Book is full of it. Books and sermons without number have been written upon it.

Why, then, a new book of sermons on conversion?

Because not all that has been written and preached on the subject is truth. Much of it is the saddest and most dangerous caricature of truth. Few subjects have been more abused, misrepresented and misunderstood. A veritable flood of ruinous error has emanated from pen and pulpit on this subject. A sad wreckage of doubt, gloom, skepticism, despair, insanity and self-destruction is the result. Much of the current twaddle is the shallowest sentimentalism or the wildest fanaticism, with all the various baseless gradations between. It tends to confuse the mind, to harden the heart, to quench the spirit, to ruin the soul.

Here, on the one hand, are our cold, humanitarian moralists. These are the apostles of culture and progress. They would evolve a dignified and proud manliness out of the natural man. Man is too great, and grand, and good, to need a re-creation—a new heart and life! Conversion, with them, is nothing but a laying aside of bad habits, an outward reformation.

On the other hand, here is a whole host of would-be evangelizers. They seem to consider it their special mission and commission to "convert sinners." They often become quite proficient in their avocation. They can bring about hundreds of conversions in an evening. They get up a revival in the home church, or start out to revive a town or city. We have heard some of them assert how they have converted whole communities, and how they were going to "capture" such a town or city "for Jesus!"

With them, conversion is a rousing of the feelings, a wave of emotion, a burst of excitement.

While they will speak in thunder tones of the necessity of conversion and of the damnation of the unconverted, they rarely even attempt to explain the nature of conversion. Ask them what it is, and they can give at best very vague and unsatisfactory answers. Ask them how it is brought about, what its agencies and instrumentalities are, and they don't know. Ask them what its evidences are, and they don't tell you. They are full of pious phrases, and earnest exhortations, and touching stories, and tearful pleadings. But the teaching of the divine Word on this all-important subject they know not!

There is still another class in the Church who need to give renewed attention to this subject.

Repelled by the fanaticism and the vagaries of the aforenamed class, they have gone to the other extreme. While the former make a hobby of the subject, these latter almost ignore it. They don't preach much conversion. They seem to be almost afraid of the term. They speak much of truth, and Grace, and faith, and righteousness. And against all this we would be the last to say one word. But to neglect or ignore the subject of conversion is certainly a very grievous and dangerous mistake. It may result in a false security in the unconverted—of whom there are certainly many among the hearers of every preacher. It may result in the loss of souls, which will be required at the pastor's hand.

In these godless and worldly times we must earnestly and diligently preach conversion. We must insist on its necessity. We must reason, exhort, convince, beseech, and plead; "*Turn ye, turn ye; why will ye die?*"

We must explain from the divine Word what is the nature of this change. We must labor to have the plainest hearer understand this vital subject and his personal relation to it. We must show how God, who alone has the power to give the new life, yet has thrown all the responsibility on man, by putting within his reach the life-bearing means of Grace.

It was the lot of the writer of this book to be

brought up in the midst of revivalistic surroundings and preaching. As a pastor also his lot has been, at times, cast among proselyting zealots. His Church, his faith, and his people, have been rudely attacked and slandered. It became necessary either to give way or to defend himself and his faith. This made it necessary to study and examine the whole subject of conversion and experimental religion. He has enjoyed the happy experience of finding that the more he studied the matter in the Word of God, the more did he discover that the Church whose name he bears holds, confesses, and teaches on this point also nothing but the pure *truth as it is in Jesus.* It has been a source of the greatest delight and comfort to discover how the scriptural doctrine meets every difficulty, clears away all doubt, harmonizes seeming contradictions between divine sovereignty and human responsibility, giving all the glory to God, and laying all the responsibility on man.

It was to help others, who perhaps had difficulties on this vital subject, that he prepared and preached the series of sermons contained in this book.

It is with the hope that they may be helpful to others also that he offers these sermons to the public. He believes that *in this direction* the field has not been overworked, and there is room for this book of sermons.

That it may help to lead some confused and groping ones into the light; that it may counteract dangerous error; that it may show the beauty, simplicity and satisfying nature of the teachings of the Word; and that it may become instrumental in leading to true conversions, is the hope and prayer of THE AUTHOR.

Fargo, Dakota, Easter, 1889.

SERMON I.

CONVERSION:
Its Nature, Necessity, and Efficient Agencies.

Acts iii. 19.

Acts iii. *19*. Be Converted.

SERMON I.

A SMALL text, but a big subject. A subject of the most vital importance. A subject round which cluster the issues of eternity.

Not only is it a subject of general interest; it is a subject of the most intense personal concern; it is a subject in which each one that reads these lines is much more deeply concerned than in the matter of making a living, getting on in the world, having a reputation in the community, or being well booked up in the questions of the day. All these questions taken together are of no weight at all when compared with the question, "How about my conversion? Am I in a converted state?" Jesus says, Matt. xviii. 3: *Except ye be converted and become as little children, ye shall not enter into the kingdom of heaven.*

Yes, dear reader, the question of your eternal weal or woe depends on the question of your conversion.

We need not stop therefore to argue that each one ought to have clear ideas on this vital subject. And yet there are few subjects on which many well meaning persons are more in the dark. Worse still, often those who talk most about it and are loudest in urging its necessity, know least about it. Why this should be so we can scarcely tell. It is certainly not because the Word of God is so misty that no one can know what it teaches. It must be because many are unwilling to search the Scriptures with a view to bow to their authority, and take their own reason captive. Too many would rather take their feelings and impulses for guides and standards, than the teachings of the Divine Word. We desire to study and examine this subject in the light of that Word, and inquire into the *nature* of this change, its *necessity* and how it is brought about, and finally some variations in the process.

If we inquire first into the meaning of the term, we find that to convert means "to turn," "to turn round," "to change about." We find this is also the clear meaning of the Latin word which is the root of the English. The same thing is true of the Greek word ($επιστρεφειν$) translated "convert" in the New Testament. Its simplest meaning is "to turn round." We, therefore, find that the same word which is in some places translated "to convert," is in other places translated "to turn."

As if a traveler discovers that he is on the wrong road, he turns, faces about, and gets on the right road—so the unconverted sinner, when he realizes that he is traveling on the broad road that leadeth to destruction, turns or is turned round, and gets on the narrow way that leadeth unto life.

If now we inquire more closely into the nature of this turning or changing about, we find that it comprises two distinct steps or parts. The first is penitence or contrition. The sinner realizes what he is, where he is, and whither he is tending. He realizes his lost and ruined and guilty state. Seeing as he never saw before the deep depravity of his own heart, the heinousness and damnableness of its sin, the justness of the judgment, and wrath to which it exposes him, he loathes that sin, he mourns over it, he desires to flee from it, and longs for deliverance. This is what the Bible calls penitence or repentance; though sometimes the word repentance is used in a broader sense, and covers the whole process of conversion. This penitence or heartfelt sorrow for sin, and earnest desire to be free from it, is the first step in conversion.

The second step is faith in Christ. The penitent heart longing for deliverance, crying out for forgiveness, has Jesus the Saviour from sin presented to it. It looks to Him. It begins to realize that He by His life and death has wrought out a complete salvation. It realizes that this Saviour has become its own substitute, borne and atoned for all its guilt. It reaches out and lays hold and casts itself upon that Saviour, and cries "*Lord, if thou wilt, thou canst make me clean,*" and then, "*Lord, I believe, help thou mine unbelief,*" and then, "*My Lord and my God.*" This is faith; it is the second step in conversion. In the first step, the sinner saw and realized that he was on the road to destruction, earnestly desired to get off that road, and began to turn his back upon it. In the second step, he saw the narrow way that leadeth unto life, and confidently set foot thereon. He is now converted or *turned from darkness to light and from the power of Satan unto God.*

Penitence then is not something that goes before conversion, and faith something that follows after, and conversion itself a mysterious something sandwiched in between; but penitence and faith are the two component parts that make up conversion. Where the former is, there the latter—unless there be a violent rupture—is sure to follow.

We inquire, in the next place, who needs this change? The self-evident answer certainly is, all who are not in a converted state; that is, all who do not have the elements or evidences of the new life in them. In other words, all who do not have in their hearts true penitence for sin, and true faith in Christ. Wherever we find true penitence and true faith, there we find a converted person; and, conversely, where these elements of the new life are wanting, there is an unconverted sinner.

Now if we look for these elementary principles of the new life, we find that there are numbers of the children and youth of Christian parents, who certainly possess them. From their earliest recollection these young disciples hated and sorrowed over their sins. From tenderest childhood they trusted in and loved the dear Saviour. They cannot think of a time when they did not love Him. These are children of the covenant. They were consecrated and given to the Saviour in tender infancy. Believing parents had them carried to the baptismal font, where, with "*the washing of regeneration,*" the "*washing of water by the word,*" they were "*born of water and of the Spirit*" in that "*baptism which doth now also save us,*" and thus "*baptized into Christ.*" This was to them the *birth*, *i. e.*, the feeble *beginning* of new life.

The germs of the new life then and there implanted by Christ's own ordinance, were afterwards carefully fostered and nurtured by the Word of God and prayer. Among the earliest conscious lessons that they learned from pious parents, were lessons about Christ and salvation and eternal life. Their parents realized that the promise is *not only to them, but also to their children*. Such children are children of the covenant. They belong to Christ since the day of their baptism. They are in line with Moses, and Samuel, and Jeremiah, and John the Baptist, and Timothy. Their mothers are in the spiritual succession of Hannah, and Elizabeth, and Lois, and Eunice.

Such children, and the youth and adults who grow from such childhood, need no conversion. They are among the best Christians, the most spiritual and consecrated disciples, the most steadfast and useful members of the Church of Christ. Oh, how many more of such, who need no conversion because they have the elements of the new life and are in a consecrated state, there might be! How many more there would be, if, in this fast age, this age of new measures, and new methods, and new experiments in the churches, so many had not drifted away from the old foundations laid in God's Word!—if a large part of what still calls itself the

Church of Jesus Christ had not repudiated the ancient Bible and church teaching concerning baptismal Grace, the baptismal covenant, prayerful home nurture, *feeding* the *lambs* in Sunday-school and Church. But, we digress.

Not all who are baptized remain true to their baptismal covenant. Largely on account of the unscriptural notions and theories indicated above, many lose or throw away the Grace conferred in baptism. They become prodigal sons, wanderers from their Father's home and protecting care. All such need conversion. As a matter of course, also, all such as have never been baptized, and know nothing of true penitence and living faith. We insist, our Lutheran Church insists, in all her standards, that all such must be converted, or they will be eternally lost.

There is absolutely no salvation, no heaven for those who remain and die in an unconverted state. Theirs is certainly a state of great peril. We inquire now how is this change brought about? What are the means or agencies through which it is wrought?

Here we remark, first of all, that no man can bring about this change by his own reason or strength. This must be accomplished, "*not by might, i. e.,* not by human might, *nor by power, but by my spirit, saith the Lord.*" "*No man can say that Jesus is the Lord, but by the Holy Ghost.*"

Conversion is a divine work. The Spirit of God must bring it about. How does He do it? Undoubtedly, through the Word. Of that Word Jesus says, "*The words that I speak unto you, they are spirit and they are life.*" The Word is the organ of the Spirit. We know of no operations of the Spirit outside of the Word. We have never heard of a person under the influence of the Spirit possessing the elements of the new life in a place where the *Word* had never gone. Only after the Word has gone into a heathen land, do we find the blessed influences of the Spirit there.

That Word calls itself a "*ministration of the Spirit,*" "*The power of God unto salvation.*" It claims to be "*quick,*" *i. e.,* living, "*and powerful, and sharper than any two-edged sword.*" "*Able to save the soul.*" It claims to have the force of "*a hammer,*" the fervency of "*a fire,*" the life of a "*seed,*" the refreshing power of "*the rain and the dew.*" It says of itself that it "*is perfect, converting the soul.*"

We find further that the same divine operations, such as *calling, enlightening, regenerating, sancti-*

fying, etc., are indiscriminately ascribed, sometimes to the Spirit and again to the Word, evidently because the Spirit is in the Word and operates through it.

This Word then is the instrument through which the Holy Spirit operates on the sinner's heart, and converts him. Penitence is generally brought about through *the law.* "*By the law is the knowledge of sin.*" It is the great preacher and producer of repentance, and thus becomes "*our schoolmaster to lead us to*—or towards—*Christ.*"

Faith is generally encouraged and developed by the Gospel. It holds up a crucified and risen Redeemer as the sinner's substitute and Saviour. It is generally while the penitent and yearning heart is contemplating the Word of the cross that "*faith cometh by hearing, and hearing by the word of God.*"

Therefore it is the Word of God as the organ and instrument of the Spirit, that converts the sinner. What a beautiful and simple method of Grace is thus presented by this true doctrine of the efficacy of the Word. The sinner cannot convert himself. What is he to do? He is to come to the Word, prayerfully read it, hear it, ponder it: he is to be careful that he resist not, nor rid himself of its divine influence. It will do its own blessed work. It will awaken a sense of sin, true sorrow therefor, earnest longing for deliverance, and finally a joyful trust and resting in Christ.

This doctrine solves and clears up and reconciles the relation of the sovereignty of God to the responsibility of the sinner. It gives all the glory to God, and yet throws all the responsibility on man. It makes the way of salvation so clear and plain that *the wayfaring man, though a fool, need not err therein.*

In conclusion we desire to notice some of the variations in the process of conversion.

Here we remark first that there is a difference in the intensity of change. Some have more intense realization and abhorrence of their sin than others. Some have a more strong and joyful faith than others. With some the feelings predominate. With others the judgment controls.

Again there are differences in the duration of the process. Some may see the awful depths of their sin and the greatness of their guilt at a glance. They may likewise see at once the availability of the salvation that is in Christ Jesus, reach out and vigorously lay hold of and rejoice in a personal Saviour. Others may be a long time in coming to a sense of sin and helplessness and need of a Saviour. The Word of God may come to them, and at first make only a slight impression, perhaps a feeling of dissatisfaction with self and a little restlessness. Little by little their eyes are opened. Message after message comes to them. Deeper and clearer do they see into their lost and ruined and guilty state. At first they see, as through a mist, the offered Saviour. Brighter and brighter shines the light from the Word of God. At first only a tremulous look to the cross, then a timid reaching forth to it, then a steadier gaze and a surer grasp and a closer approach. And so "*it shall be little by little,*" "*first the blade, then the ear, and then the full corn in the ear.*" It may be weeks or months before such persons can rest confidingly in a present and personal Saviour.

In these matters it will not do to lay down arbitrary rules. Much depends on the natural temperament of the person. One is sanguine, impulsive, hasty. In him the feelings predominate over the judgment. With such a one the change is apt to be vivid, decisive and short.

Another is of a cool, phlegmatic temperament. His feelings are not deep. He habitually weighs every matter brought to his attention most carefully.

He never gets excited or does anything hastily. In such an one the change will likely be almost imperceptible and slow. And yet, when this latter has once unreservedly accepted Christ as a personal Saviour, he is likely to be the more steadfast Christian of the two.

Again, in the work of conversion, much may depend on the former life of the person. One has wandered very far away. He has become a sinner above the Galileans. He has fallen deeply into shame and sin.

Another has not so openly and flagrantly been a sinner exceedingly before the Lord.

When the former has his eyes opened, he will be apt to be more deeply impressed with his guilt and need of a Saviour than the latter. The conversion of the one will probably be more strongly marked and sudden than the latter.

"*There are diversities of operation, but the same Spirit that worketh all in all.*" To some, the Word of God comes *like a hammer*, or, *as a fire*. On others it *drops as the rain, and distils as the dew.* Into some hearts it cuts *as the sword of the Spirit.*

They feel it *piercing even to the dividing asunder of the joints and the marrow.* Into other hearts it falls *as a seed*, and gently strikes its roots downward and sends its shoots upward. Or it is *hid* there *like leaven*, and only slowly and silently leavens the whole.

It again follows, as a matter of course, that not every one can tell the exact time when and where he was converted. Some can. Zaccheus, and Saul of Tarsus, and the Philippian jailer, and the three thousand on the day of Pentecost, and others mentioned in the Bible, doubtless could always tell. But we do not believe that the apostles of Christ could tell, neither could many others mentioned in the Bible.

Neither does the Bible anywhere demand that we should. Else what of those mentioned above, who were children of God from infancy? What of those who cannot think of a time when they did not love the dear Saviour? Shall we say: "They are still in an unconverted state?" Who will dare to say so?

To go to such a trusting child of God with such a heartless assertion, would be to confuse the mind, to burden the heart and to quench the spirit. It is by just such baseless and arrogant assertions that many a promising spiritual life has been blighted in its budding, blasted in its growing, and ruined in its fruitage. Perplexity, doubt, unbelief and despair are the baleful fruits of such anti-scripture fanaticism.

The great and momentous question for each one is not when or how were you converted, but are you now in a converted state? Do you now mourn over, hate, endeavor to be rid of and confess your sins? Do you now constantly turn to, cling to and rest on Christ as your only help and hope? Do you "*die daily*," and are you "*renewed day by day?*"

On these questions, dear reader, does your and my eternal salvation depend.

SERMON II.

THE CONVERSION OF THE WOMAN OF SAMARIA.

JOHN iv. 28, 29.

John iv. 28, 29. The woman then left her water-pot, and went her way into the city, and saith to the men: Come see a man which told me all things that ever I did: Is not this the Christ?

SERMON II.

USING these words merely as a standing point from which to look back over that whole interesting meeting and conversation between Christ and the woman of Samaria, we enter at once on the subject of her conversion.

We inquire *first*, who was this woman?

As to nationality, she was a Samaritan. As such she was a member of a despised and disreputable people.

From the seventeenth chapter of second Kings we learn that after the king of Assyria had carried captive the ten tribes, he re-peopled or colonized their land with colonies of heathen from different parts of his kingdom. These idolaters were soon troubled by lions, which the Lord sent among them as a punishment for their abominable rites. They attributed the visitation by the lions to their ignorance of the manner of the God of the land. They petitioned their king to send back a priest of Israel, that he might teach them how to propitiate "*the God of the land.*" One of the apostate priests of Israel, who had before mingled the worship of the calves at Bethel with the worship of Jehovah, was sent.

Naturally these heathen dwellers in Samaria would not learn a very pure worship of the true God. *"They feared the Lord, and served their own gods, after the manner of the nations whom they carried away from thence,"* 2 Kings xvii. 33. After the return of the Jews, when they began to rebuild the temple, these semi-idolatrous Samaritans wanted to help to build, and thus acquire rights in the new sanctuary. Ezra and the Jews wisely refused to permit such union effort. From time to time these Samaritans received renegade Israelites and profligate priests among them, and intermarried with them. By and by they built their own temple on Mount Gerizim, where they established and maintained a mongrel worship of Israel's God. Their religion was never recognized by the Jews, who treated them as even worse than heathen. To this semi-barbarous and disreputable people did this woman belong. Nationally, not a very promising subject for Grace.

But when we inquire into what she was *personally*, she becomes still less attractive. Her history was a dark one: *she had had five husbands.* What became of all of them we do not know. Worse than that, she was now living with a man who was *not her husband.* She was the mistress of a paramour! Certainly she had fallen deeply into degradation and sin. There was not much left to appeal to. If a work of Grace is to be done in her heart, the seeds will have to be sown, the life implanted and the very foundations laid. If she is converted, it will not be the return of a once regenerate and now lapsed one, but the regeneration and conversion of one dead in trespasses and sins. Will Jesus, tired, thirsty, hungry and worn as He is, pay any attention to her? Will He try to *open her eyes and turn* (or convert) *her from darkness to light and from the power of Satan to God?* Yes, He will.

We inquire, therefore, in the *second* place, how did Jesus treat her and deal with her?

As He saw her approach, He did not stop to consider her race or her character. He saw in her a *human being*, with a soul capable of being renewed into the image of God. He did not stop to reason that it would not be worth while to endeavor to enlighten and convert this single individual, when He could at any time have the multitudes to crowd round Him to hear His word. Jesus had a care for the individual. He understood that the only way to reach the masses is to reach the single soul. A lesson for all who have, or profess to have, the cure of souls.

He preached the Word to her. It pleased Him *in whom dwelt all the fulness of the God-head bodily*, who claimed that His own words *they are spirit and they are life, by the foolishness of preaching to save them that believe.* In His own practice and in His instruction and commission to His Apostles, He always went on the principle that the Word carries the Spirit and power of God, and is, therefore, the only instrument for the effectual conversion of the sinner.

Much depends on the manner of using the Word. It may be presented in such a way as to repel. Had Jesus begun by at once railing at this woman's false religion and denouncing her character, we believe she would have left Him in bitterness of heart. It is interesting and profitable to notice His method of presenting and applying that Word. He first gains her *attention*, and at the same time secures her *good will* by asking a favor of her. Having thus opened the way and in a manner put himself under obligations, He skilfully leads her thoughts from the water of Jacob's well to the *living water*, which He could give. So artlessly and yet so forcibly does He speak of that living water as the *gift of God*, and of His own ability to give it, that He wakes in her heart a vague longing.

He gives clearness and proper direction to that longing by showing her her sin. He instructs her that to get rid of this sin, it is not enough to outwardly worship in the true Church; but that she must *believe Him* and have the true spirit expressing itself in a pure worship. Thus He calls out that clear, earnest, yearning for the help of the *Messiah, which is called Christ.*

This yearning He now readily turns into a joyful faith by plainly revealing and declaring Himself as the Deliverer, the Christ whom she needs.

What lessons of pastoral theology, of true soul cure, are here! Oh, that all pastors and teachers might learn and practice them.

We proceed to notice in the *third* place how this woman was affected. And this will bring to light the process of her conversion.

We notice how, first of all, *she became interested*. She was willing to listen to and talk with this strange Teacher. This is of prime importance. We cannot expect to reach the careless sinner until we get him interested enough to gain his attention.

After her first rather frivolous question, and the earnest, lofty answer of Jesus, she became more serious. She addresses the stranger as *Sir*, *i. e.*, *Rabbi, Lord.* She inquires about this *living* water, the manner of procuring it, and the manner of person who offers it. She may not have been much in earnest as yet, still it is a point gained when we can get sinners to inquire, to ask about spiritual things.

The woman hears more about that living water and its wonderful powers to permanently satisfy. It makes her think of her own life, of its emptiness, its toil, and its weariness. She begins to experience an undefined and vague longing after something better. True, she does not yet understand what she needs. But she realizes that her life is unsatisfactory, that she *needs something*. She is thirsty.

Unexpectedly, doubtless, but very clearly, she is made to look back over her life and down into her heart. She sees the darkness of the one and the vileness of the other. One word from Him who says, "*Is not my word like a fire?*" had flashed in and shown her her shame and her sin. She felt, and winced as she felt it, that His word is indeed "*quick*," *i. e.*, a thing of life, "*and powerful and sharper than any two-edged sword, piercing even to the dividing asunder of soul and spirit, and of the joints and marrow, and is a discerner of the thoughts and intents of the heart.*" Heb. iv. 12.

Why did she ask that next question about the proper place to worship? Was it to turn aside the light of the Word, to parry its blows, to draw off her own gaze and turn aside the gaze of Jesus? Did she simply want to change the subject? Did she desire to discuss an old theological question about the *externals* of worship rather than have any further reference to her own sin and need of salvation? So many interpreters have thought, and it may be that there was something of this spirit in her question. But we cannot believe that this was all that was in that question. We believe that we must find a deeper sense in it. Otherwise Jesus would not have treated it so seriously and so instructively. Neither would a flippant and evasive question fit into the course of the narrative.

Her thirst had been intensified and properly directed. She realized her guiltiness, her need of forgiveness and change. She now had full confidence in the *wisdom* of Christ, she recognized Him as a divine *Prophet*. She wanted a sanctuary, a place where she could be certain, beyond the peradventure of a doubt, that God was present, and would attend to the worshippers. She wanted to pray, to sacrifice, to seek forgiveness and peace.

After the rather full and deep answer of Jesus,

she plaintively expresses her heart's longing for "*the Messias which is called Christ.*" Like the two disciples who afterwards walked with Him on the way to Emmaus, her *heart burned within her* as He talked with her, and she knew Him not. Her faith was not yet intelligent. But out of a penitent heart the tendrils of faith were reaching up and feeling after something to grasp and cling to. Faith was coming *by hearing, and hearing by the Word of God.*

She was now ready to hear the full Gospel, which reveals *the Messias which is called Christ.* Jesus says to her, "*I that speak to thee am He.*"

She at once recognizes and accepts Him as the Christ, her Saviour. And is not this true faith? Does any one doubt it? If so, see how that faith at once proved itself.

She immediately left her water-pot—she forgot, for a time, her temporal affairs. She had found better water than that in Jacob's well.

Like the disciples, when they recognized the call of Jesus, they left their boats and fishing-nets. Like Matthew, who on a similar occasion left the receipt of customs, so this new disciple leaves her water-pot.

She hurries into her city, where she is well

known. She turns evangelist. She invites the men to "*come.*" She tells them of the Christ whom she has found. She makes known to them that He "*told her all she ever did.*" Thereby she confesses her sin, and expresses her penitence. She assures them that this is the Christ. Thus she professes her faith, and thus her faith is beautifully bearing fruit. She is truly converted. Her conversion becomes the occasion of many others. As in David's time, "*Then will I teach transgressors thy ways and sinners shall be converted unto thee.*" Jesus remains two days in that city, reaps a glorious harvest there. During these two days He no doubt further instructs the woman of Samaria, and her faith becomes more intelligent.

A few closing reflections. This was the conversion of a bad woman. Let no one say that such or such a one is a hopeless case. Let no sinner say, "My case is hopeless." He can and does, *save to the uttermost, all that come unto God through Him.*

This conversion was brought about by the Word. So is every true conversion. Its elements were penitence and faith. These are the component elements of every conversion.

Reader, are you converted? Have you in your heart true sorrow for and hatred of sin? Do your sins trouble you? Do you *die daily?* Are you constantly turning to Him and resting in Him who is the Christ, the Saviour of the world? Are you in an unconverted state? Can you and do you laugh at your sins? Are they as trifles to you? Would you be converted? Come to the Word! Hear it. Read it. Ponder it. It will bring about, if prayerfully used and not resisted, a vivid sense of your lost, ruined and guilty state. It will also beget a saving and appropriating faith in Christ.

"*Turn you, turn you; for why will you die?*"

> Beside the well at noon-tide
>   I hear a sad one say,
> "I want that living water,
>   Give me to drink, I pray;
>
> The well is deep, O Pilgrim,
>   But deeper is my need;
> I thirst for Life eternal
>   The 'Gift of God' indeed."
>
> Ho every one that thirsteth,
>   The living water buy!
> Ye blessed ones that hunger,
>   Take eat, and never die.

SERMON III.

THE CONVERSION OF THE PRODIGAL SON.

LUKE xv. 17-20.

Luke xv. *17-20.* And when he came to himself, he said, How many hired servants of my father's have bread enough and to spare, and I perish with hunger. I will arise and go to my father, and will say unto him, Father, I have sinned against heaven, and before thee, and am no more worthy to be called thy son: make me as one of thy hired servants. And he arose, and came to his father.

SERMON III.

Somebody has said: "If I could have only one book of the Bible, and had my choice, I would select as that book the Gospel of St. Luke." When asked why he would select this book above all others, he said: "Because of the fifteenth chapter."

We cannot find much fault with this choice. This is indeed a rich and precious chapter. Its three parables are radiant with the reflections of the glowing love of the Father's heart.

If it were possible to narrow down the choice still more closely, and where all is so supremely excellent to select the most excellent, we would unhesitatingly select the parabolic story of the wandering, returning and welcomed prodigal. This parable has well been called "the Gospel in the Gospel"—the Gospel in a nutshell.

The whole parable naturally divides itself into two parts: First, the part that delineates the younger son; and second, the part that portrays the elder son.

The former part again naturally subdivides itself into three parts. The first shows us the wilful departure from a loving parent and good home of the wayward youth. It pictures to us the wilful departure of the sinner from God. The second portrays the wanderer's return, portraying for us the sinner's conversion. The third part paints in vivid colors the reception of the returning one.

We propose to consider more particularly the second point, viz: the prodigal's return, or conversion; for a turning round, or returning, is a conversion. Before entering upon the process of the conversion itself, we would further remark, that this conversion differs from some others recorded in the New Testament. This is the returning of one who once enjoyed a good home, a father's love and care. He had a birth-right in that home, but renounced it and the father who gave it. The father, however, had not yet renounced him.

In the case of the Samaritan woman, we had the conversion of one who, as far as we know, had never had a birth-right in a spiritual home. She had always been a stranger to the covenant and an alien from the household of faith. Hers was the regeneration and conversion of a sinner: this is rather the conversion or restoration of a once regenerate, but now lapsed one. That was the bringing to God for the first time of a sinner: this is the coming back of a wanderer who was once baptized into Christ, enjoyed some Christian nurture, and was, perhaps, confirmed in the church.

We would further note, as preliminary to the exposition that particular parables are intended to bring out and specially portray different phases or features of the same truth. Some, *e. g.*, that of the great supper, are intended to show more especially the part that God works in the bringing back of the sinner. Others, as the one before us, are intended to emphasize the process in the sinner, and the manner of its manifestation. The divine side, the efforts and means of Grace, are, therefore, only incidentally shown.

Turning now to the conversion of the prodigal, we divide the process into three steps.

The first step was: *He began to think.* Theretofore he didn't want to think. If a reproachful thought, or a memory of the past, would occasionally flit through his mind, he made positive efforts to shake it off. It was, doubtless, partly to prevent or drown all sober, serious thought, that he plunged so heedlessly into dissipation. Thinking would disturb his wild enjoyment. It would make him uneasy. It would rob him of what he called his peace. And, therefore, he did not wish to think.

Is it not always thus? Will any wilful, wayward wanderer sit down quietly and think of himself, his life, and his God? Dare he? No. On the contrary, he will use every endeavor to prevent serious thought, or to banish it, when it comes unbidden.

But God was training that prodigal. He desired to make him think. He permitted him, or may we not say He led him, to taste the bitter fruits of his own sin.

He began to be in want. This was intended to make him pause and think. So God often disciplines the sinner. He sends privations, losses, disappointments, diseases or death. These afflictive dispensations are not in themselves means of Grace. They do not carry saving virtue. But they are intended to prepare the careless for the reception of the means of Grace. They are designed to make the thoughtless think.

He came to himself. He had been *beside* himself. The inconsiderate and careless sinner is not in his right mind. When he has been made willing to consider, to think, to remember, then he comes to himself, and in coming to himself, he is beginning to come to his God.

Look at that prodigal! He has come to want. He is herding swine. He is hungry. He craves *the husks*, the pods of the carob-tree, on which the swine are feeding. He begins to consider the situation. He looks at himself. He is covered with rags and filth. He looks over his life. What a loving father gave, he has *wasted in riotous living*. He looks into his heart. He sees its vileness and its ungrateful meanness. His thoughts go back to what he once was. He recalls his home. That father-heart and father-love—those fatherly counsels and admonitions! He remembers it all. He thinks it all over.

Here we *incidentally* see that it is the work of *the Word*. And it is thus the sinner is brought to himself. He remembers that he was baptized into Christ, and set apart for the kingdom of God. He recalls the holy lessons he once learned and loved. He recollects the prayers, the counsels and admonitions of years gone by. He contrasts with all that his present life, his heart, his whole self. He is coming to himself. He is beginning to think. An important point is gained. He has taken the first step in his conversion.

We do not know how long the prodigal had been thinking, or how long he had fought against sober, serious thought. It may have been many days since he began. It may have been very reluctant and timid thinking at first. It may have been weeks and months since the first serious and unwelcome thought had crossed his mind. Little by little, in quietness and alone, he pondered, till at last he fully *came to himself.* The first step was taken.

The second step in his conversion was that *he began to feel.*

We hear him talking to himself. He speaks of his own unworthiness. With him these are not mere words. In public, men often make confessions and acknowledgments for effect. They are mere words. Not so with him who is alone, who is musing out of a full heart, whose heart is so full that his lips speak almost unconsciously. He can say: *While I mused the fire burned.*

The prodigal felt his unworthiness, his ungratefulness, his meanness. He loathed himself. He felt he was vile. He also felt the load and burden of guilt. *I have sinned,* sinned *against heaven,* am guilty in God's sight; I deserve punishment, *am no more worthy to be called a son,* forfeited my sonship, sold my birthright, deserve to be cast out, disinherited, disowned. These, we believe, were the feelings of his heart. It was a true mourning over sin. It was *godly sorrow, working that repentance that needeth not to be repented of.* He was a penitent, and penitence is the first part of conversion. It manifested itself in his case in first thinking of the father, his love and his counsels. He then thought of himself, his heart and his life. He contrasted self with the father and the father's word. He saw his sin. His thinking made him *feel.* It awoke a consciousness of unworthiness and self-abhorrence. It made him feel his guilt and the deservedness of punishment. This is God's way of dealing with the sinner. He makes him think, thinking leads to feeling, the heart is reached through the head, the judgment is informed, and through it the conscience stirred and the heart moved. When Paul was sent to convert the Gentiles, he was commissioned "*to open their eyes and to turn*—*i. e.* to convert—*them from darkness to light.*" The first thing then was to open their eyes, *i. e.* to enlighten or instruct them; and this is the only true way. Instruction must come first. There must be knowledge, something to think about; then the feeling will come of its own accord. Those who would begin with the feelings, who aim to arouse and excite the sinner whom they desire to convert, are beginning at the wrong end. They are proceeding in a method that is contrary to the laws of the mind, as well as contrary to the Word of God. Rational feeling is the product of rational thinking.

We go on to notice the third and final step in the prodigal's conversion. *He began to turn.*

In all his wanderings he had been turned away from his father and away from his real self. He was unwilling to turn even his thoughts back to his father or in on himself. But now he was turning. His thoughts were looking homeward and inward. His feelings also, so deep within him, were beginning to reach out toward his home. His heart was yearning for that father's pardon and love.

As he thought and longed, he remembered his father's goodness. He became convinced that the father was merciful. His heart reached out towards that mercy; it grasped it and was ready to throw itself upon it. He had no self-justification. He pleaded no excuse or extenuation. He didn't say he would go back and say he couldn't help it, it was the fault of others who led him astray. No, no; he frames no plea for self, he trusts only in the father's *mercy*, he wants only *pardon*. He rises, he turns, he hastens to receive that pardon.

And what is this turning towards the mercy of the father? What is it but *faith?* Yes, it is the outgrowth of penitence, and that is always faith; and penitence and faith together are conversion. The prodigal has turned to his father. His turning is believing. Where there is believing there is conversion.

Look at it.

It began in pondering the blessings and counsels of his home days. The *Word* of our heavenly Father, even when silently pondered, is a means of Grace, a bearer of the Spirit.

His thinking wrought feelings of unworthiness; a sense of guilt; a hatred of his sin, and a longing for deliverance.

This turned his thought and heart to his father; it made him lay hold of the remembered mercy; it made him *arise and go.* It brought him to his father.

The thoughts and feelings of his heart were al-already framed in words for his lips. *He confesses:* true faith always confesses. *With the heart man believeth unto righteousness, and with the mouth confession is made unto salvation.*

Look at the reception of the returning one. Will the father receive him? He comes in rags and filth. He carries the handwriting of sin on his countenance. The mark of Cain is there. He looks degraded and vile. Will not the father shut the door in his face? Will he not tell him, "You made your bed, now lie in it?" Will he do like many an earthly father has done? Look and see. The old father has been waiting and watching. *When he is yet a great way off*, the father sees him; he runs to meet him; *he falls on his neck; he kisses him;* he calls him "*my son!*"

Oh yes, the son had tried to forget the father, but the father had not for a moment forgotten or disowned the son. The baptized one may forget, he may repudiate his side of the covenant, but God never forgets or breaks His side. He is ever ready to welcome back the penitent one; to give him the kiss of forgiveness; to own him as "*my son*," "*my daughter.*"

Notice how eagerly the two come together. On the part of the son, there is no struggling, no wrestling, no pleading, no penitential season of waiting, and working, and getting through. On the part of the father, no holding back, no barring of the door, no refusing to hear or to heed, no reluctant opening at last, because the son is about ready to frantically break in. Surely no modern revivalist drew that picture!

Dear reader: Are you a wanderer? Are you now away from the Father-home and Father-heart? Are you sojourning in that *far country*, that wild, waste land, where God is not? Is there sometimes a thought of former and better days—a pang of home-sickness? Do you sometimes realize that you are *in want?* Do you perhaps recall the prayers once, in the dim and distant past, lisped at a mother's knee? Do there come at times echoes of the stories and sayings of Jesus, which then fell into eager ears and a receptive heart? Do there flit occasionally across memory's canvas, unsought images of childhood's Lord's Days, of the walk to the Sunday-school, of the teacher, the lessons, the hymns and prayers? Do you see again the sainted pastor, and hear again those words that then were sacred with a heavenly sound? Has the church-bell ever startled you? Does the sight of others going joyfully to the sanctuary of God make you restless? Oh, do not shake off these serious impressions. Cherish them! Take down the old Bible and catechism: begin to think; think till you feel; feel till you loathe yourself, and long for deliverance. Look then to mercy as it shines from the cross. Turn to the Crucified; there the Father will meet you. He is waiting. He is coming to meet you. He is standing before you. Accept Him. Receive His advances. Call Him Father. He calls you son. He kisses you with the kiss of pardon and adoption.

> Come home! Come home!
> You are weary at heart,
> For the way has been dark,
> And so lonely and wild.
> O Prodigal Child, come home!
>
> Come home! Come home!
> From the sorrow and blame,
> From the sin and the shame
> And the tempter that smiled.
> O Prodigal Child, come home!
>
> Come home! Come home!
> There is bread and to spare,
> And a warm welcome there.
> Then, to friends reconciled,
> O Prodigal Child, come home!

SERMON IV.

THE CONVERSION OF THE PUBLICAN.

LUKE xviii. 13.

Luke xviii. *13*.   And the publican standing afar off, would not lift up so much as his eyes unto heaven; but smote upon his breast, saying, God be merciful unto me a sinner.

SERMON IV.

We have before us a character sketch, drawn by a master hand. With a few words, two representative persons, quite opposite in heart and life, are made to stand before us in life-like colors. It is a double picture, drawn by Him who could portray the inner and outer man as none else can, because *He knew what was in man, and needed not that any one should tell Him.*

It is no wonder that those writers who have best succeeded in delineating human nature—as *c. g.* Shakespeare—have been close students of the Bible. No other book uncovers and lays bare the secret springs of the human heart like this book. No other master can portray the hidden impulses and motives of humanity like He who made man. For the same reason none else could so truthfully and vividly show the out-workings and manifestations of the spirit within.

He *in whom dwelt all the fulness of the God-head bodily*, has with a few master strokes, drawn for us the pictures of the Pharisee and the Publican. These pictures are set before us for our instruction and profit. We are to contemplate them. We are to be warned by the one: we are to be instructed and drawn to imitation by the other.

We desire for the present to look more particularly at the second picture, and consider *the conversion of the publican.*

We will consider first one of the greatest hinderances to conversion—we mean *self-righteousness.* We see this delineated and manifested in the Pharisee. We, therefore, study him as contrasted with the Publican. The Pharisee is self-righteousness personified. We see it standing before us. We see how it lives and moves and exalts itself toward heaven. We see what it is and whence it springs.

It is a complacent satisfaction with self. It is an unctuous self-flattery. It is a magnifying of one's supposed virtues. It is a wilful blindness to one's own faults. It is greatest in negative virtues. Its passive virtues are trifles magnified. Look at and listen to that Pharisee. He goes up to the temple, he considers himself a religious man, he professes *to pray;* but what a prayer! There is no word of confession, except a confession of other people's sins. There is no breath of petition. He stands forth boldly and prominently. He begins with thanksgiving, but he does not thank for mercy, for Grace, for blessings received; he is so full of self and self-sufficiency, that he can only thank for what he is and what he does, in contrast with others. He delights to compare himself with the common herd. He first tells the Lord what he does not do. He is not an extortioner. He is in no sense unjust. He is too pure to ever be capable of committing adultery. He can best sum up his goodness by thanking the Lord he is not *like this Publican*. Such is self-righteousness, a fearful disease of fallen humanity, one of the greatest hinderances to its restoration.

It is well that we understand this disease. There are few places in the Word of God that so clearly describe it, as does this parable. It will be profitable for us to look into it a little more deeply.

What are the *roots* of self-righteousness? There are two main roots. One is a shallow view of God and His law. The other is a superficial understanding of sin and self.

This was the trouble with this Pharisee, and indeed with all the Pharisees of Christ's day. He did not realize the august, sublime and holy nature of the Being whom he so bluntly and boldly addressed. Had he had even a faint conception of

Him *whose eyes are like flames of fire, too pure to behold iniquity or look upon sin with allowance*—had he understood even remotely, how the very nature of God shrinks from and abhors sin, that He is so inexpressibly pure that He *charges His angels with folly, and that the very heavens are unclean in His sight*—had he even approximately known that the whole past history of Israel, the whole service of that temple in which he stood, was intended to teach God's holiness—had he, in short, understood the nature of God, he could not have done as he did.

Because he did not understand God's nature, therefore, he did not at all know God's law. In boasting of his own good deeds, which he doubtless regarded as a fulfilling of the law, there is not a word of *fearing, loving or trusting in God*. Indeed, the whole first table is deliberately passed over. He flatters himself that he has kept the law because he has abstained from the gross acts of extortion, adultery and injustice. He mentions *two* positive virtues. He boasts of these as marks of supererogation, as doing even more than the law demanded. Had he heard and understood the Sermon on the Mount, he could not have imagined that he kept the law.

Because he did not understand the spirit of the law, therefore, he did not know what sin is. To him sin consisted in the outward acts of the hand, the tongue, the stomach, or other bodily organs. He did not realize that sin is really a matter of the heart and spirit. He had not learned that *lust* or desire is sin. Had he known what sin is, in its essence and nature, he would not have dared to so stand before God. Knowing not what sin is, he had no conception of the sinfulness and desperate wickedness of his own heart. He did not know himself. Thus his ignorance of God and His law, and his ignorance of self and sin, made him self-righteous.

Self-righteousness was the greatest obstacle our Saviour had to contend with. It was characteristic of the Scribes and Pharisees. He could reach and gather in Publicans. and sinners, but He reached very few Pharisees. To them He said: "*The Publicans and harlots go into the kingdom of God before you.*"

Self-righteousness is the great obstacle to the Church's progress to-day. Our age is sadly afflicted with this malady. It has crept into many popular churches. The holiness of God and the sinfulness of sin are too little understood and realized. Consequently Christ is too little appreciated. Repentance and faith are not preached as they should be. Superficial expedients are tried to gather in sinners. Self-righteousness is not exposed and dislodged. True conversions are comparatively rare.

The Church can stoop down and pick up the fallen out of the filth and mire of sin, when such are brought to realize their sin. But the Church cannot reach, Christ cannot save men, as long as they *trust in themselves that they are righteous, and despise others.*

The only remedy for this dire malady is the Word of God. That *sword of the Spirit* must cut in and lay bare the corruption and soreness of the *deceitful and desperately wicked* heart. It must *pierce even to the dividing asunder of the joints and marrow, and discern the thoughts and intents of the heart.* "*By the law is the knowledge of sin.*" Through the Word the Holy Spirit *convinces the world of sin, of righteousness and of judgment.*

This living Word, carrying the Spirit's life, had certainly done its preparatory work in the heart of the Publican, to whom we now turn.

We believe that we see in him a product of the power of the Word. It had prepared his heart: although our parable does not definitely mention this, we reason from the effect to the cause. It was now converting that heart. We see in that heart the workings first of *penitence* and then of *faith.* Notice the penitence as manifested first in his *actions.*

He *stood afar off.* He felt himself unfit to approach too near the Holy place—like some outcast, coming into a church and standing by the door, as if too base to enter farther into the house of God.

How opposite to the Pharisee, who stood forth conspicuously, doubtless as near the Holiest place as possible!

He *would not so much as lift his eyes unto heaven.* Unworthy and ashamed to look up, he casts his eyes upon the ground. Ashamed because of his sin, bowed down with a sense of guilt, his very attitude is a confession of sin and sorrow therefor.

Blessed shame! It is a hopeful symptom. The blush of shame because of sin, has well been called the morning dawn of a new life. Ezra said: "*I am ashamed, and blush to lift up my face unto Thee.*" Job said: "*I am vile.*" Jeremiah complained of the impenitent Jews: "*They were not at all ashamed, neither could they blush.*" And again: "*Thou hadst a whore's forehead, thou refusedst to be ashamed.*"

The Publican *smote upon his breast.* As if to indicate, "here is the sore spot, here is the impure heart, here is the seat of sin." To him sin did not consist in a few outward acts. To him it was, first of all, a diseased and defiled condition of his very being. It was not so much the sins of the hand or tongue that worried him, but the sinful heart from which those sprung. *He smote upon his breast.*

By this he further indicated that he *deserved* smiting. As a transgressor, he felt guilty. As guilty, he felt worthy of stripes. As justly subject to punishment, *he smote upon his breast.* His actions betokened penitence.

So did his *words.* He designates himself :"a *sinner.*" More literally translated, *the* sinner, or *the sinful one.* As though he had been a sinner above all others. As though he had been the only one. Here was a strong confession of individual and personal guilt. It was more than a general confession of general sinfulness. It was self-condemnation. It expressed in words what had been shown in acts.

This singling of himself out as the chief of sinners is the very essence of a thorough repentance. When the sinner sees himself as standing apart from a sinful race, as justly condemned for personal guilt, then has he been enlightened from on high, *convinced of sin* by the Spirit of God.

It is this sense of personal guilt and condemnation to which all must come. There is no true conversion without it. A general confession is easily made. It is not so hard to believe that all are sinners. But it is quite another matter to realize and feel, "*I* am a sinner," "I am *the* sinner," "I am the *chief* of sinners," "Sin in the abstract has become *concrete* in me." Such was the Publican's confession. He was truly penitent.

But his penitence grew into *faith*. True penitence is the root of faith, and true faith is the fruit of penitence.

We see his faith in his plea for *mercy*. Like the penitent prodigal, when he thinks of his father, he remembers and ponders the one trait of mercy—so this Publican. His eye is cast down, but his bowed heart cries upward. He calls to mind that God is merciful. His heart yearns for mercy. While his mind thinks of mercy, his heart reaches out for it.

Mercy is something unmerited. It cannot indeed be earned. What is earned or paid for cannot be mercy. It cannot be bought. It can only be received as a free gift. Faith is a turning towards and laying hold of mercy. Self-righteousness asks for rights. It demands wages. It wants justice.

Faith claims nothing as a right. It asks not for wages. It seeks not justice. Faith knows that to ask for justice is to ask for rejection, to claim wages earned is to claim condemnation.

In the days of Napoleon the Great, a timid little girl once pressed her way through the courtiers and stood before him. Looking down into her pleading face, the emperor said, "Well, child, what is it?" Tremblingly she told him that she came to beg for the life of her father, who was under sentence of death. Growing stern, the emperor replied, "Child, your petition is useless: twice before your father deserved death, and was pardoned, and now *justice!* justice to my country, and justice to myself, demands that he suffer the penalty." "Sir," said the little pleader, "I come not to ask for *justice*, but to beg for *mercy*."

And so the Publican came. And so must every penitent come. And so does true faith ever come. It sees the proffered mercy. It realizes that it is unmerited and free. It reaches out towards that mercy. It grasps it, it clings to it, it casts itself upon it, it rests there. This is faith. The Publican is converted.

Sinner, there is mercy for you. You cannot earn it. It has been earned, by the obedient life, the atoning death and triumphant resurrection and ascension of our Lord and Saviour, Jesus Christ. You cannot buy it. It has been bought and paid for by Him. You cannot prepare yourself for it. You need only let Him prepare you, by coming to that living Word, which will convict you of your guilt, your need, your own helplessness, and the abounding help of free mercy. It will enable you to lay hold of and rejoice in that mercy.

The Publican went down to his house *justified*. He was justified, not because he had made himself worthy, but because he believed. *"A man is not justified by the works of the law, but by the faith of Jesus Christ . . . for by the works of the law shall no flesh be justified. Being justified by faith, he had peace with God through our Lord Jesus Christ."*

It was a blessed church-going to him. Every church-going ought to be attended with the same blessed results. Oh, for a congregation of worshippers with hearts bowed down with a sense of sin, emptied of self-sufficiency, yearning for richer measures of Grace, and believing that Jesus does furnish that satisfying Grace.

One of our old German ministers was once congratulated by a Presbyterian pastor on his large audiences and general popularity. "Oh, no," said the old Lutheran, "I have nothing yet to be congratulated on. My people don't realize yet that without Christ they are all poor, lost and ruined sinners." May our church-going be always so blessed to us, that each attendance may deepen our penitence and increase our faith.

> All that I was, my sin, my guilt,
>   My death, was all my own.
> All that I am I owe to Thee,
>   My gracious God, alone.
>
> The evil of my former state
>   Was mine, and only mine,
> The good in which I now rejoice
>   Is Thine and only Thine.
>
> Thy Grace first made me feel my sin,
>   It taught me to believe,
> Then, in believing, peace I found,
>   And now I live, I live!

SERMON V.

THE CONVERSION OF ZACCHEUS.

LUKE xix. 2-9.

Luke xix. *2-9.* And Jesus entered and passed through Jericho. And, behold, there was a man named Zaccheus, which was the chief among the publicans, and he was rich. And he sought to see Jesus who He was; and could not for the press, because he was little of stature. And he ran before and climbed into a sycamore tree to see Him; for He was to pass that way. And when Jesus came to the place, He looked up, and saw him, and said unto him, Zaccheus, make haste and come down; for to-day I must abide at thy house. And he made haste, and came down, and received Him joyfully. And when they saw it, they all murmured, saying, That He was gone to be guest with a man that is a sinner. And Zaccheus stood, and said unto the Lord: Behold, Lord, the half of my goods I give to the poor; and if I have taken anything from any man by false accusation, I restore him four-fold. And Jesus said unto him: This day is salvation come to this house, forasmuch as he also is a son of Abraham.

SERMON V.

ZACCHEUS was a publican. The publicans were the tax collectors among the Jews of our Saviour's day. The tax, or tribute as they called it, was levied by Rome. Though conquered by Rome and under its rule, the Jews fretted under the yoke and yielded only a sullen and unwilling obedience to its authority. They hated to pay tribute to Cæsar, and consequently hated those who collected the tax. And so every one hated the sight of a publican.

The Roman government took contracts for the taxes. For example, some rich man would become responsible for the taxes of a certain district or county. He would sub-let that district to a number of others, each one of whom became responsible to him for a certain section, as *e. g.* a township. The sub-contractor again would generally hire men to go from house to house and gather in the money. Thus it came about that the tax money had to pass through three or four hands before it reached the treasury of Rome. Each one of these hands wanted a profit. In order to make a profit more tax was collected than was levied by Rome. And so it became almost a part of the system to extort unlawful money. The people knew this, and therefore hated these unjust and oppressive publicans still more. To be a publican was, in the eyes of the people, to be an extortioner. Those who had the contracts for larger districts, were *chief among the publicans.* Such was Zaccheus.

The city of Jericho was probably the most important commercial city in Palestine. Lying just opposite the fords of the river Jordan, it was on the great highway that led from Arabia and Assyria across into Egypt. This City of Palm Trees was naturally a headquarters for those who were chief of the publicans. Zaccheus lived there.

Our text gives us an account of the remarkable conversion of this chief publican. It is this conversion that we now desire to consider.

We inquire, first: *What led to that conversion?* There are some who tell us that it was the curiosity of Zaccheus that led to his conversion. They say that he had heard about Jesus, and therefore had that curious desire to see Him that we all have to look upon some eminent or famous person. And this idle curiosity alone, they tell us, made him so eager to see Jesus.

We confess that this strikes us as a rather superficial view of the matter. To us the eagerness of Zaccheus seems too great to be accounted for on the mere ground of curiosity. There seems to be a deep and intense earnestness underlying his rather strange actions. The sequel of the story also seems to squarely contradict the idea of a mere curiosity.

We believe there were deeper motives there. We believe that prevenient Grace was at work there.

Jesus was closing up His public ministry. He was on His last journey to Jerusalem. For three years He had been going up and down in the land with blessings in His heart, with blessings on His lips, and with blessings in His hands. He had been the great Helper and Healer of the bodies and souls of men.

His fame had gone abroad into all the land. Everywhere people were talking about Him. He had been in the region of Jericho at different times before. Zaccheus must have heard about Him. The tax-collectors under him, who were going from house to house, among the people, would naturally come in contact with some who had seen and heard Jesus, who had been helped, or had seen others helped. Quite likely some of these under-publicans had themselves seen some of those wonderful deeds of love, and heard some of those wonderful words of life. All this they would report to Zaccheus when they came to pay over their money. They would also be very likely to tell him that this wonderful Jesus did not think Himself above speaking to, mingling with, and helping men of their own despised class—that He had even called one, who had been a chief among the publicans, from the receipt of custom, to become one of His twelve disciples.

Zaccheus heard these stories about Jesus. This was *Gospel* to him, for what is the Gospel but the glad tidings, the good news of the Son of God? Zaccheus had this Gospel only in disconnected stories and rumors. It was only a fragmentary Gospel, but it was all the Gospel he had. And even this Gospel was to him *the power of God unto salvation.*

He had accepted that Gospel. He had believed those stories. They had stirred in him longings after a better life. They had worked an earnest desire to come near to this Jesus and receive a blessing from Him. His heart was going out towards this unknown Jesus.

Here let us notice, in passing, that Zaccheus might have resisted, and shaken off these impressions; he might have plunged more deeply into business and speculation; he might have *quenched the Spirit*, who was working through the Word— but he did not. He allowed that fragmentary Word to do its blessed preparatory work. This led to his conversion.

We notice, *secondly, the obstacles in the way of his conversion.*

First: *He was rich.* Riches have ever proved a formidable obstacle to the conversion of sinners. God demands the whole heart or none. He will not have a divided heart. We *cannot serve God and Mammon.* Riches take a strong hold on the human heart. Covetousness grows as wealth increases. "*Take heed, and beware of covetousness,*" "*which is idolatry.*"

In the chapter preceding our text we have a sad example of the adverse power of riches. In view of that example Jesus said: *How hardly shall they that have riches enter into the kingdom of God! It is easier for a camel to go through a needle's eye, than for a rich man to enter into the kingdom of God.* Further on He explains that while *with man it is impossible, with God it is possible.* It seems to require a special measure of Grace from God, and special earnestness on the part of himself, for a rich man to become and remain a child of God. Zaccheus was rich. Here was an obstacle to his conversion.

Again, there was a bodily impediment, *he was small of stature*—so small that he could not see Jesus for the crowd that surrounded Him. This physical disability might have kept him away from Jesus. He might have said, "I want to see Jesus, I had fully intended to see Him; but my smallness of stature prevents me, and so I'll give it up."

A further difficulty in the way was the ridicule to which he would expose himself by taking a position where he could see. As a publican he was despised by the people. He knew that they would be only too ready to ridicule him if he should climb into that tree. Again, he had a certain dignity to maintain. He was a *rich* man, a *chief* among the publicans, an officer of the Roman government; and should he so compromise his dignity as to make a public spectacle of himself? Should he run ahead of the crowd, and in full view of them, climb into a tree like a boy? Should he become a laughing-stock to his enemies and a mortification to his friends? Here were obstacles to overcome.

But Zaccheus was too much in earnest to be deterred. Oh, how many have been kept away from Christ by just such impediments as were in his way. How many have had their first serious thoughts, their first good impulses, checked by *the deceitfulness of riches*. How many have been kept out of the kingdom of Grace here, and the kingdom of Glory there, by the glitter of gold. Not so Zaccheus, he was already beginning to *esteem the reproach of Christ greater riches than the treasures* of Rome.

And how many again have been kept out by bodily impediments. Oh, how many are kept away, or rather keep themselves away, from the house of God and the means of Grace, by real or imaginary bodily ailments. Alas, these nervous spells! These Sunday headaches! This dread of exposure on the Lord's day! We have known many who could work hard all week, but were too weak or nervous or sick to go to church on Sunday; because of slight or only supposed bodily ills, the poor soul was allowed to starve and die.

On the other hand, we have known persons who really had serious bodily ailments, who yet had themselves led or carried into the house of God. We have seen persons sit under the preaching of the Word, while their bodies were shaking with pain. These were in earnest. They were hungry. They wanted to meet Jesus in His Church and in His ordinances. Such was Zaccheus. Too little to see Jesus like other people, he quickly devised a way and found a place where he could.

How many also have been kept from yielding to the strivings of the Spirit in the preaching of the Word, because they were afraid of ridicule. Alas for the number that have been laughed and sneered out of heaven. Zaccheus did not stop for this, but boldly braved the bravado of the crowd. Thus he overcame every obstacle that stood in the way of his conversion.

In the *third* place we notice *the conversion itself.*

We have already noticed the preparatory work that had been done by the fragmentary Gospel he had doubtless received. Through this the preparatory Grace had reached him, and drawn him towards Jesus. This had brought him to where the Word and look of Jesus could reach him. And Jesus did reach him. He looked up and saw him. As an old writer says, "He saw in Zaccheus a ripe fig, ready to drop into His lap." It was there, in that tree, where the turning point was made. There the decisive step was taken, and Zaccheus was converted.

When Jesus spoke to him, called him by name, and bade him to come down, it was the same voice, the same living Word that had spoken power into a withered hand, and life into dead bodies.

Zaccheus heard that Word. He yielded fully to its power, and in yielding he *turned from darkness to light, and from the power of Satan to God.* When Zaccheus *made haste and came down*, he was a converted man.

How far the beginnings, that led to that final step, lay back, we do not know. Doubtless the beginnings were small. A passing thought about Jesus, a timid look into his own heart, a hasty glance over his past life, a slight dissatisfaction with self, an unexpressed longing after something better—such may have been the beginnings. It was the seed-corn, rooting and sprouting. With clearer ideas of sin and the Saviour, with deeper sorrow for sin and more earnest longing to come to this Saviour, the change was becoming more decisive. And now the crisis had come, and he surrendered fully to Christ. The great rending choice was made.

Let no one despise the day of small things. Where small measures and opportunities of Grace are improved, greater ones are given. Let it also be still borne in mind, that even now Zaccheus might have refused to come down and receive Jesus into his house. He might have resisted even this effectual call. Man always has the sad and awful prerogative and power to beat back the hand that is stretched out to save him.

In conclusion, we notice the evidences that Zaccheus was truly converted. A true conversion always proves itself. So did this one. Zaccheus made a public confession. This must follow every conversion. "*With the heart man believeth unto righteousness, but with the mouth confession is made unto salvation.*" Zaccheus confessed his former sins. He did this in the presence of the people, and before Christ.

He said, "*If I have taken anything from any man by false accusation.*" This is at least an acknowledgment that he had not been careful to be honest, that he had been capable of taking by false accusation. Thus he confessed his sinfulness and his sin.

He confessed Christ by coming down from the tree at His call, going with Him in presence of the murmuring crowd, and making this public declaration to Him as his *Lord*.

He further proved his conversion by his determination to make restitution for any wrong done. A truly converted man cannot keep what he knows is ill-gotten gain. His enlightened and now tender conscience, compels him to make restoration as far as possible.

In purposing to make restitution, Zaccheus, at the same time, professed that henceforth he would be strictly honest in all his dealings. There can be honesty where there is no religion, but there certainly can be no true religion where there is no honesty. A true Christian cannot misrepresent, adulterate, give short weight, or measure or take advantage of ignorance, in his business transactions. A man may pray ever so fervently in prayer-meeting, or talk ever so touchingly in experience meeting, but if he is not strictly truthful and honest in all his dealings, we take no stock in his religion. A true conversion turns a dishonest into an honest man.

Again, Zaccheus became liberal. Half of his goods he determined to give to the poor. A true conversion turns the stingy into the liberal man. It opens the pocket-book as well as the heart. There is no such thing as a Christian miser. If one is a miser he is not a Christian, he needs to be converted.

Finally, salvation came to *the house* of Zaccheus. not that all the members of the household were at once converted, but the head of the family had become a disciple of Christ. This brought a Christian atmosphere into the home. The Word of God and prayer took their proper place in the family. The things of God were talked about and taught in the household. A true conversion shows piety at home. We once heard a boy say with considerable bitterness: "Yes, my father can pray at prayer-meeting, but I never heard him pray at home." He professed to be a Christian, but salvation had not been brought by him into the house.

Behold then, in Zaccheus, the proofs of conversion. Do you profess to be in a converted state? Can you show the evidence that he showed?

Are you still unconverted; *in the gall of bitterness and the bond of iniquity?* Would you be converted? What must you do? Simply *use the means*. Use them diligently and prayerfully, and they will bring renewing Grace into your soul.

SERMON VI

THE FALL AND RECONVERSION OF PETER.

MATT. xxvi. 69-75.

Matt. xxvi. *69–75*. Now Peter sat without in the palace: and a damsel came unto him, saying: Thou also wast with Jesus of Galilee.

But he denied before them all, saying: I know not what thou sayest.

And when he was gone out into the porch, another maid saw him, and said unto them that were there: This fellow was also with Jesus of Nazareth.

And again he denied with an oath, I do not know the man.

And after a while came unto him they that stood by, and said to Peter: Surely thou also art one of them; for thy speech bewrayeth thee.

Then began he to curse and to swear, saying: I know not the man. And immediately the cock crew.

And Peter remembered the word of Jesus. Before the cock crow thou shalt deny me thrice. And he went out and wept bitterly.

SERMON VI.

AMONG all the interesting characters of the New Testament, there are none more interesting than the Apostle Peter. There is something about him that invites study. There is much in him that is fascinating. We often feel that we cannot help but love him. On the other hand, he often vexes us. His character requires careful and unprejudiced examination. If we fail to understand the whole man, if we stop short of considering his whole career, we will be quite likely to form a one-sided judgment. There is danger of making him either a hero or a coward. Before we can understand his fall and recovery, we must understand the man.

Peter, with his younger brother Andrew, was among the earliest of Christ's followers. He had been a disciple of John the Baptist, by whom he had been directed to Jesus. Jesus at once took particular notice of him and paid special attention to him. His name had been Simon; Jesus changed it to Cephas, which is the Syriac word for *Petros*, which is the Greek word for rock. "*And when*

Jesus beheld him, he said, Thou art Simon the son of Jona: thou shalt be called Cephas, which is by interpretation, A stone." John i. 42.

From among the large number of disciples, Jesus selected twelve to be apostles. It seems that Peter was the first chosen; his name is always mentioned first in the lists of the apostles. From the beginning he was a recognized leader. By common consent he acted as the spokesman for the rest. He was one of the favored three who stood closest to Jesus; they were permitted to witness miracles that none others saw; they were with Jesus on the mount of transfiguration; they with Andrew heard that long, deep and thrilling prophecy concerning the destruction of Jerusalem and the end of the world. Jesus certainly recognized Peter as a true disciple; he was neither a formalist nor a hypocrite. Not only did he witness good lip-confessions, but Jesus said to him, Matt. xvi. 17, *"Blessed art thou, Simon Bar-jona: for flesh and blood hath not revealed it unto thee, but my Father which is in heaven."*

We notice some elements of strength in his character. The first is the conviction of his own sin. On one occasion when he was suddenly confronted with the power and divinity of his Lord, he vehemently confessed, *"I am a sinful man, O Lord."*

This we consider an element of strength. In the kingdom of Grace there is no strength without a sense of sin and unworthiness. He who most clearly and most fully realizes this has in him the foundation of the greatest strength. Paul, who could say "*of whom*—i. e. of *sinners*—*I am chief*" could also say, "*when I am weak, then am I strong.*"

Again we recognize his strength in his clear and unreserved confession of Christ, or his faith. When "*many of His disciples went back and walked no more with Him, then said Jesus unto the twelve, Will ye also go away? Then Simon Peter answered and said, Lord, to whom shall we go? Thou hast the words of eternal life.*" John vi. 66–68. And so again when Jesus asked, Matt. xvi. 15, 16: "*But whom say ye that I am? And Simon Peter answered and said, Thou art the Christ, the Son of the living God.*"

We see a further element of strength in his deep *love* for his Lord. When he recognized Jesus walking on the water, he at once desired to get near to Him. "*Lord, if it be thou, bid me come to thee.*" When Jesus announced that one of them should betray Him, Peter became very solicitious for his Master. When told that *all* should *be of-*

fended because of Him, Peter violently protested, that for his part, he was ready *to go to prison and to death* with Jesus. Neither was there any intended hypocrisy in this. Peter spoke as he felt; he did love his Saviour; he did on the first approach of violence draw his sword and begin to fight for Him. There is no doubt but that even some of his blunders were in part the expressions of unreasoning and impulsive love. So, on the mount, when *he wist not what he said*, and proposed to *build three tabernacles* because it was *good to be there*, there was in it a desire to remain near Jesus. So again when he rebuked his Lord for intimating His approaching sufferings and death, there was doubtless love in his hasty words; and so also when he protested against Jesus washing his feet.

But there was also some self-love present. Peter had his weak side; it showed itself again and again. It culminated in his sad deep fall.

Peter was too much guided by impulse; He was too much a man of feeling; he acted too much on the spur of the moment; he was too hasty; he was inconsiderate; he spoke without thinking; he was *swift to speak* and *slow* to hear; he was willing to build towers without counting the cost; ready to go on a warfare on his own charges. We see this in nearly all his actions; we hear it in most of his words. When he started so boldly to go to Jesus on the water, he soon began to look on the winds and waves, and *began to sink*. Instead of asking Jesus for instruction concerning His sufferings and death, he presumed to *rebuke* the Lord, and thus drew upon himself the severest rebuke that Jesus ever gave to a disciple. Before he understands or tries to understand the foot-washing, he breaks out, "*Thou shalt never wash my feet.*" Before Jesus gets through explaining it, he flies to the other extreme and gives the Lord directions: "*Lord, not my feet only, but my hands and my head.*" He hasn't the patience to sit still in the darkness and watch, as directed; but after each plaintive plea from Jesus, he goes to sleep. But without being bidden, he draws his sword and blindly smites and threatens to make more mischief for the Master. Self-love also sounds through his rebuke of the Lord and his transfiguration speech; he wanted an earthly kingdom and a place in it. For this he was willing to smite with the sword; for this he was asking when he said "*Behold, we have forsaken all and followed thee: what shall we have therefor?*"

We naturally inquire into the underlying causes of these weaknesses and contradictions in Peter.

From what we have already noticed and from other instances and glimpses of Peter, we believe we can safely infer that he did not understand the mission of Jesus. Together with nearly all the people of his day, the enemies as well as the friends of Jesus, Peter believed that it was the mission of the Messiah to deliver Israel from the Roman rule and re-establish the throne of David and Solomon. In this sense Peter also "*trusted that it was He which should redeem Israel.*" To *redeem* Israel was to break the power of Rome and make of Israel a great and glorious nation. Peter had laid hold of this idea with all the ardor and enthusiasm of his impulsive nature. What a kingdom that would be with "*the Son of the living God*" on the throne! And what privileges and prerogatives for those who should be *great* or favored by being near the King! This he thought was coming on the mount. For this he was willing to draw the sword, to brave the prison and the death.

But when Jesus so earnestly set His face toward Jerusalem, when on that momentous journey He so solemnly repeated the predictions of His suffering and death, Peter was shocked, he was bewildered, he was offended, he refused to give up his favorite idea—he didn't want a *suffering* Saviour. He had made up his mind that it should not be. His mind thus pre-occupied and pre-determined, he was not in a teachable frame. And though Jesus spoke plainly and repeated His instructions, Peter *understood not;* he didn't want it so, and therefore persuaded himself that it would not be so—that there must be some hidden meaning in the words of Christ. And so Peter remained in ignorance; he did not understand that Jesus must first be our Priest to offer up Himself as the Lamb of God for the sins of the world; he did not understand that His kingdom must be built on His Priesthood. He did not understand the principal lesson which Jesus as a prophet had come to teach, viz., the nature of His Priesthood and its necessity in the sinfulness of man.

Oh, how hard it is to unlearn an error when that error is congenial and well-pleasing to the reason and the desires of the natural heart! How hard to accept a truth when that truth is above reason, and makes the proud reason bow in child-like submission, and when it is contrary to the desires of the natural heart and condemns that heart and its desires as sinful and guilty of wrath!

We might go a step further in Peter's case, and affirm that Peter did not understand the vicarious work of Jesus, because he didn't understand himself. He didn't have a full and clear conception of the sinful and utterly ruined state of his own heart. He was conscious of a certain enthusiastic devotion to Jesus. He further believed that his salvation *in some way* depended on fellowship with this Jesus. But had he fully known the depravity, the deceitfulness, the lurking roots of treachery that lay hidden there, he would have had a deeper penitence and a more clinging faith. He would have felt that he needed first of all a sacrifice for sin, that there could be no kingdom for him without this. Peter lacked in *intelligent* conviction. His feeling was not the outgrowth of knowledge. Instead of being guided by principle, based on understanding of self, and of his Master, he was guided too much by impulse.

How important to be carefully instructed in the truth! How necessary to have clear ideas of God's way of salvation! How indispensable for safety and strength, especially in our dangerous age, to have piety built on principle, principle on conviction, and conviction on clear conceptions of God's truth. The most glowing spurts of enthusiasm, the most fervid feelings of love, cannot dispense with the necessity of instruction. We still need the catechism.

To return to Peter. We are now ready to understand his shameful fall.

He had followed after Jesus to the High Priest's palace. John had procured him admittance into the open court in the centre of the palace. The room in which the trial of Jesus was going on, opened on this court-yard by a hallway or porch. Those that were without could see and hear all that was going on within. Peter was first accosted by a portress who kept the gate. To her he made a simple denial. The second time he was more closely questioned by another servant-maid of the High Priest, who charged him more directly and more publicly with being a follower of Jesus. "*And again he denied with an oath, I do not know the man.*" About an hour afterwards he was still more forcibly accused by a kinsman of Malchus. Others that stood by joined in the charge, and told him that his very speech or dialect betrayed him. And now comes the lowest step. "*Then began he to curse and to swear, saying, I know not the man.*"

What a fall was that for a disciple! And that disciple Peter! And Peter all this time in the presence of Jesus! And all this only a few hours after that earnest warning, "*Simon, Simon, Satan hath desired to have thee, that he may sift thee as wheat!*"

A few hours after that clear prediction, meant to prevent the denial: "*Before the cock crow twice thou shalt deny me thrice.*" And those tender words "*But I have prayed for thee.*" And that confident boasting, "*Though all should be offended, yet will not I.*" "*I am ready to go with thee to prison and to death!*" We are shocked at Peter! We are ready to hold up our hands in holy horror! We are eager to hurl our anathemas at the miscreant!

Let us not be hasty. We have before us the natural manifestations of the remains of "*the old man, which is corrupt according to the deceitful lusts.*" We all carry the remnants of that same old nature. Let us *not be high-minded, but fear.*

We have looked into the character of Peter, and seen in it the remote causes that led to that sad fall. There were also immediate causes.

We have already seen that Peter did not know himself. Therefore, he did not mistrust himself. On the other hand, he had a large amount of self-confidence. Jesus had several times on that eventful night exhorted him to "*watch and pray that ye enter not into temptation: the spirit indeed is willing, but the flesh is weak.*" Peter did not feel himself weak, and therefore, after each exhortation to *watch, he had gone to sleep.* Had Peter watched and prayed in the garden as directed, he would have been stronger when he came to the High Priest's palace. Had he not trusted too much in self, he probably would not have slept away those momentous hours when his Redeemer was crushed to the earth under the load of man's sin.

Here was an immediate cause of his fall.

Another cause, closely connected with this one, was his running needless risks. He had not been told to follow Jesus to the trial. He had been clearly told that he could not and should not interfere to help his Master. His duty, for the present, was to let matters take their course.

But he went to the palace. He mingled freely with the enemies of his Lord. He sat down among them and warmed himself by their fire. What a place for an apostle who had no mission there and no motive but *to see the end*.

Ah, Peter! Better would it have been for you, one of the keenest smarts would have been spared the Master, if you had waited at a distance till He had again required your service! They that rush needlessly and heedlessly into danger have no right to count on divine protection.

What a terrible weapon is ridicule! How many disciples have done like Peter! Uncalled by duty, and not for the sake of doing good, they have mingled with the enemies of their Lord. They have warmed themselves at the coal-fires of the world. They *walk in the counsels of the ungodly, stand in the way of sinners, and sit in the seat of the scornful.* The finger of scorn is pointed at them. They wilt, and shamefully *deny the Lord that bought them.*

Beware of bad company!

But we hasten to notice the recovery or re-conversion of Peter.

What brought it about? The crowing of the cock, say some. Such expounders tell us that a thunder-storm, a grievous loss, a sad disappointment, the news of an accident, or the sight of a funeral, has converted many a sinner. We do not believe it. Neither the crowing of a cock, nor a fright, nor an affliction of any kind, is in itself a means of Grace. These things do not carry renewing or sanctifying power. They are of use only in so far as they make one think, as they direct attention to, call to mind, and drive to *the Word and the sacraments.* These are God's means of Grace. They carry His Spirit, His life, and His power.

So it was with Peter. He hadn't noticed or paid attention to the first crowing; but now that crowing startled him, it recalled the Word. Then *Peter remembered the word of Jesus.* That Word was *the sword of the Spirit.* It cut down, it showed Peter his awful sin.

Thus do the providences of God bring the sinner to the Word and the Word does its own blessed work. Where there is or never has been a Word of God, there all the providences have never converted a single soul.

As the Word pierced Peter's heart, he looked and saw Jesus *turned* and looking at him. Had Jesus turned permanently away from Peter, would Peter ever have really turned to Him? We believe not. In this case also He turned to Peter before Peter turned to Him. God always comes first to us.

That look of Jesus, so full of grief, and compassion, and yearning! Oh! how it went to Peter's heart. It recalled still more forcibly His Word.

It was enough; Peter did not resist that Word. It did its own blessed work. *Peter went out and wept bitterly.* All his bravado was gone. All his self-trust had vanished; he was humbled into the dust. His heart cried out, "I am *vile.*" "*I loathe myself.*" He was truly penitent.

But his penitence grew into faith. Had it not,

it would have turned to despair. His heart turned back to Jesus; eagerly, restlessly, sadly, and no doubt prayerfully, he awaited events. On the morning of the resurrection, he, with John, was the first man at the tomb; he was the first to enter into the sepulchre. Surely his faith had again turned to Jesus; he was again converted. Jesus sent to him His first personal message by the women; and Peter was the first apostle to have a private interview with his risen Lord. Jesus had predicted his conversion or turning back, and now the prediction was fulfilled.

From the example of Peter "*let him that thinketh he standeth, take heed lest he fall,*" and let him who has fallen, learn how to rise again.

SERMON VII.

THE CONVERSION OF THE DYING THIEF.

LUKE xxiii. 39-44.

Luke xxiii. *39-44*.   And one of the malefactors which were hanged railed on Him, saying, If thou be Christ, save Thyself and us.

But the other answering him, rebuked him, saying, Dost not thou fear God, seeing thou art in the same condemnation? And we indeed justly; for we receive the due reward of our deeds; but this man hath done nothing amiss.

And he said unto Jesus, Lord, remember me when thou comest into (in) thy kingdom.

And Jesus said unto him, Verily I say unto thee, to-day shalt thou be with me in paradise.

SERMON VII.

The scene of our text is laid amid the most tragic and exciting surroundings.

A little outside of the city of Jerusalem, just beyond its north wall, is a bare elevation, overlooking the city and its temple. An immense and excited crowd of people are gathered there. It is a mixed multitude. The rabble from the streets of Jerusalem are there. The small traffickers who have come to the city to make money off the Passover crowd are there. The villagers and peasants of Judea and Galilee and remoter parts are there, come to Jerusalem to keep the feast of the Passover. The officials and dignitaries of the temple, the religious rulers and teachers of the people, the Scribes and Pharisees, the chief priests and elders are there.

In the centre of that surging and boisterous mass of humanity is a band of Roman soldiers. In the midst of that band stand three crosses, and on them hang the naked victims, enduring the intensest agony and the fiercest tortures.

And who is that central figure, so different from

the others? What means that sublime appearance, that look of heaven on His face, though marred with anguish and blood? Let us look on in reverence and adoration. It is the Lamb of God on the self-chosen altar of sacrifice, making expiation for the sins of the world.

We desire at present to look more particularly at one of the other victims. They are called *malefactors* or *thieves*—more literally, robbers. Probably men like Barabbas, who had been engaged in revolt against the Roman government, and had been guilty of robbery and murder.

The one is well-known to us by the name "The Dying Thief," or "The Penitent Malefactor."

His sudden penitence and conversion have afforded matter for much speculation. They have been made the basis of dangerous errors and soul-destroying practices.

It is well then for us to carefully and prayerfully study that remarkable conversion. We naturally look *first* for the cause of that change of heart. What was it that so powerfully influenced that criminal and softened his heart?

There are some who believe that he had come in contact with Jesus, or at least heard about Him in former times; that if he had not himself witnessed

His blameless and benevolent life, seen some of His mighty works and heard some of His life-giving words, others had told him of these things. There seems to be some ground for this position in the words "*this man hath done nothing amiss.*"

But this is at best an inference, and we cannot build positively on it.

But we do know that this man had been led out from the hall of Pontius Pilate, through the streets of Jerusalem and up to Gabbatha, in company with Jesus. The *title*, "*This is Jesus the King of the Jews,*" had been either carried ahead or hung to the neck of Jesus. This alone was enough to make that man, in whom all seriousness and right feeling had not yet been crushed, think. He had noticed the strange calm dignity, the unearthly demeanor, the heavenly look of this fellow prisoner. He had heard and seen the bitter lamentations of the women for Jesus. He had heard those awful, searching and prophetic words from the thorn-crowned Jesus: "*Daughters of Jerusalem, weep not for me, but weep for yourselves, and for your children. For, behold, the days are coming in the which they shall say, Blessed are the barren and the wombs that never bare, and the paps which never gave suck. Then shall they begin to say to the mountains, Fall on us; and to the hills, Cover us. For if they do these things in a green tree, what shall be done in the dry.*"

Pregnant words! Fearful warning! Words peculiarly *quick and powerful and sharper than any two-edged sword, piercing even to the dividing asunder of the joints and marrow, and discerners of the thoughts and intents of the heart.*

This malefactor had heard the taunts and jeers of the crowd. And from these bitter scoffings he learned what Jesus had claimed for Himself, that He was "*the Christ*," "*the Son of God*," that He "SAVED *others.*"

In the midst of their fiendish insults and injuries Jesus had calmly prayed, "*Father, forgive them, for they know not what they do.*" How confidently this Sufferer cast those breaking eyes upward and called God "*Father!*" What divine love and compassion breathed forth in that petition! And all this the thief had heard and seen. Had he not had enough of that "*engrafted Word which is able to save the soul?*"

Doubtless the Divine Spirit was at work. Through the spoken and the embodied Word. That Spirit was convincing him of his own *sin*, of Christ's *righteousness*, and of a *judgment* which threatened him, but from which the *righteousness* of this Divine Sufferer could save him. Thus was he brought to that true *repentance that needeth not to be repented of.*

We notice briefly, in the next place, the manifestation of his penitence.

From the accounts of the two former evangelists it appears that he had even joined in, probably very feebly, with the railings of his fellow criminal. That very railing may have been an unintentional expression of the struggle and restlessness within his own breast. At any rate, he immediately repented of having said even an unguarded word against Jesus.

And now, when his companion again breaks out in bitter scoffing, he openly rebukes him, and at the same time gives expression to the deep penitence of his own heart.

He publicly confesses that they are having to do with *God*—that they have every reason to *fear*, and that they are under *condemnation.*

Thus does he publicly confess his own guilt, without extenuation or palliation. He recognizes indeed they are *justly* under condemnation, *for we receive the* DUE REWARD *of our deeds.*

Here indeed we see the very essence of true *pen-*

itence. Here is undoubted evidence of a work of Grace. The sinner, in his natural state, can never thus realize his own ruined and condemned state, and the righteousness of whatever punishment God sees fit to lay upon him. When these symptoms appear, then the Holy Spirit is doing His own blessed work. That warning to his brother sinner, that solicitude lest he plunge himself still deeper into the abyss of suicidal impenitence, that warning to stop, to turn, to recognize who it is at whom he is railing—all that also proves his penitence.

As soon as the sinner is really concerned about his own salvation, just so soon does he become anxious for the safety of others.

We notice in the *third* place the faith of this penitent one.

He sees in Christ a holy, a sinless one, who has *done nothing amiss.* He confesses that Jesus "*knew no sin.*" He acknowledges and addresses Him as "*Lord.*" He believes that this Lord has a *kingdom* at His disposal. He believes that He has power to help, and that His power extends beyond the grave. He believes that this King not only can but *will* save him. Therefore he turns to Him. He addresses to Him that humble yet large petition.

In that petition he claims no merit. He pleads not that *because of* his own suffering, because of his own faith in the midst of unbelief, because of his confession in the midst of denial, that *therefore* the Lord should save him.

Oh, how many there are who comfort themselves with the idea that *because* they have had such a hard time in this world, because they have suffered so much, *therefore* the Lord will surely save them. Thus they would make a merit out of the suffering which they often bring upon themselves by their sin. Or they make a *merit* out of their faith. They flatter themselves that God *owes* them salvation, that they have *earned* it by believing.

But faith earns no merit. It is only the beggar's hand that reaches out to receive the free gift. The malefactor makes no plea for self. He simply asks to be *remembered*. And thereby he bases his entire hope on Christ's merit and mediation. It is not faith in self, but faith in Christ.

This has been called the brightest example of faith in the whole Bible, and there is ground for such a claim.

Look at the situation. Jesus of Nazareth was hanging helpless in His blood. He was dying a felon's death. He had been tried by His own people, condemned as a deceiver and blasphemer. The public teachers of the Jews, the guardians of the faith and of the temple, repudiated and spurned Him. His own followers, who had professed implicit confidence in Him and His kingdom, had also given Him up and forsaken Him.

In the face of all this, this man believes in Him. He sees Him hanging there, and on His bowed head there rests a crown of thorns. Yet he believes that to Him belongs a crown of glory, and the throne of the universe! Those eyes are filming in death, yet he believes that He is the Prince of Life and can give eternal life to all who believe. Those hands are now nailed fast, yet he believes that they can distribute the amnesties and endowments of heaven.

Surely, from that malefactor's cross there shines a faith that is radiant with the reflection from the Redeemer's cross. Surely this dying thief is well-fitted to be the first trophy of the cross of Christ. Lord, give us such a faith as this!

And that faith is accepted. Jesus immediately responds, "*Verily, I say unto thee, To-day thou shalt be with me in Paradise.*" Had the penitent prayed "*Remember me?*" Jesus answers, "*Thou shalt be with me.*" Instead of getting merely a concern in thought, he gets a place with Jesus "*in Paradise.*" The prayer looked to an indefinite future, "*when thou comest in thy kingdom.*" The answer is "*to-day,*" not in the distant future,. thou shalt be with Me.

Jesus always gives to the prayer of faith, *far more exceedingly above all that we can ask or think.* The promise is to Jerusalem, *i. e.*, to all the believing, that "*she hath received of the Lord's hand* DOUBLE *for all her sins.*"

We notice here, in passing, how the word of Christ to the penitent malefactor disposes of the old heresy lately again so prominently and boldly put forth by certain Adventists and other sects, that the soul does not live between the death and resurrection of the body. If we had no other passage on the subject but this one, it alone would give the lie to all soul-sleeper heresies. But besides this passage, we have the clear declaration of Christ, when speaking of the *God of Abraham and of Isaac and of Jacob*, He says that *God is not the God of the dead but of the living.* We have the actual appearance of Moses and Elias recorded; one as a glorified body and one a disembodied spirit, showing clearly that there is a soul-life and a body-life beyond this world. Then we have also the narrative of the rich man and Lazarus. All which agrees with Christ's words here and with Paul's expression that *to be absent from the body is to be present with the Lord.* This is the teaching of the Word from beginning to end.

Our passage likewise effectually disposes of the figment of a purgatory. If there were such a place where the sins of this life are to be purged by fire, there could have been no fitter case or place than this to set it forth.

We desire to offer a few reflections in closing. We have here a case of true conversion. There is no room for the least doubt about its genuineness. It was also most certainly a conversion in the last hour of life and in full view of death.

These are facts. There is nothing to be gained by denying them or explaining them away. These facts have however been used as the basis of unwarranted conclusions. They have been made the basis of soul-destroying doctrines and practices. They have been so used, or rather *abused*, as if they were written for the special purpose of encouraging the putting off of repentance to a dying day. This is certainly an inference without the shadow of a support, either in this narrative or in any part of the Bible. It is an inference inspired from beneath.

The teaching of the Word is, "To-day, *if you will hear his voice, harden not your hearts.*" "Now *is the accepted time;*" "Now *is the day of salvation;*" "*If thou hadst known, at least in this thy day, the things that belong unto thy peace.*" To him who did postpone and say to his soul, "*Soul, thou hast much goods laid up for many days,*" God said, "*Thou fool, this night shall thy soul be required of thee.*"

At the very most this incident teaches that it is barely possible to be saved in a dying hour. An old writer has well said, "we have this *one* case that no penitent sinner may despair, *only* one that no sinner may presume." The Bible covers a history of nearly four thousand years, and yet it has only this one instance of a dying man's conversion. And even this case certainly was not one who had deliberately planned to postpone attention to his soul's salvation to a dying day. In all probability this was the *first time* that Christ and His Word were ever brought home to this criminal. It is quite likely a parallel case with those eleventh hour laborers who could truly say, "*no man hath hired us.*" Certainly no parallel to those who deliberately and with purpose slight every call from God's Word, wilfully shake off every impression from above, grieve away the Spirit of God, and say, "I'll wait till I'm old or threatened with death." What must be the state of heart at which such arrive? What must be the withering and hardening influence of madly saying, "I'll first grind out the corn of life; I'll use all the good meal for self, and then I'll offer the bran to God." For such persons there is not a single promise in the Bible. They can certainly extort no consolation from the story of the dying thief. The Grace of God in Christ Jesus can truly save to the uttermost *all who come to God, i. e.*, all who come by the one way of genuine penitence and faith. But the probabilities all favor the supposition that those who wilfully neglect and resist the means of Grace and postpone repentance to a dying day will never come to true penitence and faith. Like Jerusalem, these things will be "hid from their eyes." So-called death-bed conversions are nearly all spurious.

Again it has been said, "this man was saved without baptism, without the Lord's Supper, without belonging to church." Probably this is all true; but it by no means follows from this, as some would have it, that therefore the Church and the sacraments are of no consequence. To say this is to charge our Saviour with folly. *He* said, "*I will build my Church."* He instituted the sacraments and made them binding on His Church till He would come again. He connected promises and Grace with His own sacraments. Now if, after all, one is just as well off without as with them, then our Saviour made a great mistake.

But the dying thief was saved without them. Yes, for the simple and very good reason that he could not obtain them. Had they been available, doubtless he would most thankfully and devoutly have used them. But as he could not have them, God in mercy took the desire for the deed, and conveyed His saving Grace through the oral Word, without the Sacramental Word.

Our Lutheran confessions and theologians clearly and tersely state the teaching of the Word on the necessity of the Sacraments when they say "not the *absence* but the *contempt* of the sacraments condemns."

With those who could have the sacraments of Christ and the privileges of the Church, but neglect them, it is *contempt* of what God has ordained as channels of Grace. And such can extract no justification of their course and no hope of salvation from the conversion and salvation of the penitent malefactor.

How sad that men will *wrest* even the most precious portions of *the Scriptures to their own destruction*, and thus turn what was intended as *a savor of life unto life* into *a savor of death unto death.*

> There is a fountain filled with blood
>   Drawn from Immanuel's veins,
> And sinners plunged beneath that flood,
>   Lose all their guilty stains.
>
> The dying thief rejoiced to see
>   That fountain in his day,
> And there may I, as vile as he,
>   Wash all my sins away.

SERMON VIII.

Tests and Fruits of a True Conversion as seen in Peter's Reinstatement into the Apostleship.

JOHN xxi. 15–20.

John xxi. *15-20.* So when they had dined, Jesus saith to Simon Peter, Simon, son of Jonas, lovest thou me more than these? He saith unto him, Yea, Lord; thou knowest that I love thee. He saith unto him, Feed my lambs.

He saith to him again, the second time, Simon, son of Jonas, lovest thou me? He saith unto him, Yea, Lord; thou knowest that I love thee. He saith unto him, Feed my sheep.

He saith unto him the third time, Simon, son of Jonas, lovest thou me? Peter was grieved, because he said unto him the third time, Lovest thou me? And he said unto him, Lord, thou knowest all things; thou knowest that I love thee. Jesus saith unto him, Feed my sheep.

Verily, verily, I say unto thee, when thou wast young, thou girdedst thyself, and walkedst whither thou wouldst: but when thou shalt be old, thou shalt stretch forth thy hands, and another shall gird thee, and carry thee whither thou wouldst not.

This spoke he, signifying by what death he should glorify God. And when he had spoken this he saith unto him, Follow me.

SERMON VIII.

In a former discourse we considered the Fall and Re-conversion of Peter.

We saw how after all the admonitions, warnings, and prayers of Jesus, after all his self-confident boasting, Peter shamefully denied his Lord. He denied Him three times.

We saw further how the crowing of the cock brought to Peter's remembrance the Word of the Lord, and how that Word fell *like a hammer* and *burned like a fire*. We saw Peter deeply penitent in his bitter tears. We saw again how Peter did not, like Judas, turn his back entirely on Jesus and give way to despair. But even as Jesus had turned upon Peter a look of sorrow, compassion, and love, so Peter turned his penitent heart towards Jesus, and yearned for forgiveness and restoration. We noticed how anxiously Peter awaited further developments, how he was early at the sepulchre, was the first man to enter in and see the abandoned grave-clothes of his dear Lord, and was the first apostle to have a private interview with the risen Jesus. Thus did Peter show his faith. He was turned back again, re-converted.

At that private interview on the afternoon of Resurrection day, Peter no doubt made full confession, and Jesus granted full absolution.

On the evening of the same day also, Jesus met the ten apostles in that upper chamber. Peter was one of them. There Jesus recognized the apostleship of all of them by His emphatic words: *"Peace be unto you: as my Father hath sent me, even so send I you. And when he had said this, he breathed on them, and saith unto them, Receive ye the Holy Ghost. Whosoever sins ye remit, they are remitted unto them; and whosoever sins ye retain, they are retained."*

Thus had Jesus, on the very day of the Resurrection, recognized the apostleship of Peter. But notwithstanding this, it was due to Peter, and it was due to the other apostles, that before Jesus reascended to His Father, Peter should make a special and public profession and receive a special and public commission. It is this special profession and commission of Peter that is recorded in our text. In this deeply interesting scene Jesus brings out and shows us the *Tests and Fruits of a true Conversion.*

We notice *first* how skilfully and yet how forcibly Jesus reminds Peter of his sin. It is well to be reminded often of weakness and sin. Such reminders are calculated to keep believers humble, to make them more watchful and prayerful, to incline them to a more diligent use of the means of Grace, and in every way to keep them closer to Christ. Such reminders are also very good tests of spiritual life. Those who have little or no spiritual life, grow impatient under such reminders. The self-righteous become angry and turn away from him who shows and recalls their sin. But a true Christian, one who has in him the elements of the new life, viz., penitence and faith, grows humble and prayerful and pure under them. Thus it was with Peter.

That night of fruitless toil and that miraculous draught at Jesus' word would naturally recall to Peter that similar night and miracle three years before. It would remind him how, at that time, he was clearly called into the apostolic band to be a "*fisher of men.*" It would naturally bring up the reflection: "How unworthy of my office and calling have I proved."

And then that "*fire of coals,*" how naturally would it recall that coal-fire in the court-yard of the high priest's palace!

But when Jesus asked that question *three* times

over, then would Peter keenly feel the reminder to the *thrice repeated* denial.

And in that searching question Jesus never calls him *Peter*, but only *Simon, son of Jonas*. This was his old name; the name by which he was known when he plied his trade as a fisherman, and knew not Jesus. When he became a disciple Jesus had said: "*Thou shalt be called Cephas, which is, by interpretation, a stone.*" After this he was generally known by that new name, either the Syriac *Cephas* or the Greek *Petros*, which reminded him of his new life and destiny. But here Jesus addresses him every time by the old earthly name, as if to say "Where is that Cephas, that rock which seemed so firm? Is not all that professed strength and stability gone? Is it not merely the son of Jonas that is left?" Peter doubtless felt the reminder, and smarted under it. He was *grieved.*

Still further, that first question inquired not merely after some love, but after a special, a superior love. Lovest thou me *more than these?* Again Peter would recollect how he had claimed superior devotion. He had put himself above all the rest. "*Though all should be offended, yet will not I.*" Where was that *more* love?

Thus did Jesus probe that hitherto wayward, impulsive, and self-confident apostle. Thus did He test the sincerity and the genuineness of that penitence. Thus did He, at the same time, *deepen* that godly sorrow, and gently draw it more into that *repentance to salvation, not to be repented of.*

Jesus was also testing and developing Peter's faith. Was Peter's faith strong enough to admit and bow to the authority of Jesus to thus examine and probe him? Did Peter believe that this Questioner examined not merely with words, but that He searched the heart, that He looked in upon the hidden springs and motives and desires of the inmost soul? Peter's faith stood the severe test. He not only recognized the authority of Jesus, but clearly confessed His divine omniscience when he said "*Lord, thou knowest all things; thou knowest that I love thee.*" Peter's faith was not only tested and proved, but in the testing his faith was developed and strengthened.

The penitence and faith of Peter were proved. The new life was there. Peter was again in a converted state.

But Jesus does still more. He wants to lay bare that which is the very breath of the new life. This leads us to notice *secondly* how Jesus probes for *Love.*

Jesus had certainly loved all the disciples. But to Peter He had granted special manifestations of love. How had He not borne with his waywardness! How often He had reached out to restrain and uphold the impulsive one! How patiently He had instructed him! How earnestly He had admonished and warned him! How gently He had led him! How tenderly He had prayed for him! How freely He had forgiven him!

It is in the very nature of love to demand love. Scarcely anything is so hard to bear as unreciprocated love. Therefore Jesus asks for Peter's love. Therefore those earnest, searching questions. Jesus wants to know from Peter whether that heart of his is really attached to Him, whether it yearns for Him, whether it pants for Him "*as the hart panteth after the water-brooks.*" Jesus wants to see whether that heart beats warm for Him, whether it longs for closer fellowship and communion; whether it eagerly responds to His approach, and hears music in His name and words. Jesus wants the warm, fervent, glowing feelings of the heart for Himself.

Ah! yes; Jesus demands real love from all who would be His. As we shall see in a moment, Jesus is not satisfied with a religion that is *all* feeling and nothing but feeling. But, on the other hand, let it never be forgotten that the Word of God nowhere recognizes a religion *without* feeling. There is no such thing as a cold-hearted, loveless Christian. Feeling has its place in true religion. It is a vital part of genuine piety. It is not the beginning of the new life. It does not come first in conversion. It is not the first step in a return towards God. The first element of an inner, spiritual life is penitence, the next is faith; these two belong together. They are the new life. But after penitence has begun and grown into faith, then love is sure to be present. It is the inner witness, the manifestation, the very breath of the new life. *Lovest thou me?* was asked of Peter. *Lovest thou me?* is asked of every one who professes to be *turned from darkness to light and from the power of Satan to God.*

That the love which Jesus demands is not a mere sentiment is seen in its outward manifestations. We might call these the fruits which grow on the tree of love, which again springs from the roots of penitence and faith.

This brings us to notice *thirdly*, how Jesus brings out and shows *the fruits of love*.

We have seen that love is the vital breath of the

new life; that it manifests itself in the inner life; that its seat is in the emotional part of our nature; that we love with the heart.

But this love of the heart manifests itself or shows itself in the outward life. It dare not remain confined in the heart. Jesus does not recognize a secret love. He knew that Peter had love in his heart; but that love is to be called out; it is to prove itself. And now we shall see how clearly Jesus teaches that *mere* feeling is not enough.

First: That love of the heart must be confessed by the lips. Peter must speak it out three times. Peter is to be taught that public confession is necessary. He is to be taught further that such confession is to be made not only before the friends of Jesus, but also before His enemies. Peter had heretofore more than once witnessed a good confession before Jesus and the other disciples. That is not so hard to do. It is easy to confess the sentiments of those around us. But Peter had proved insufficient to confess before enemies. He is now to learn that his love is to be strong enough to confess that faith before bitter and angry foes. His love is to enable him to declare his convictions before chief priests, and scribes, and elders, and a howling mob. How nobly did Peter's love afterwards bear this fruit. When arrested, tried before the Sanhedrin, charged to cease preaching Jesus and the resurrection, and threatened with dire punishment in case of disobedience, Peter boldly challanged them and said: "*Whether it be right in the sight of God, to hearken unto you more than unto God, judge ye. For we cannot but speak the things which we have seen and heard.*" Acts iv. 19, 20.

The love of the heart must speak from the lips, even before enemies. Again: Love shows itself in service. True love is not only willing but glad to labor for the loved one. Therefore, every time that Peter professed to love, Jesus bade him prove that love by labor. "*Feed my lambs. Feed my sheep.*"

Lovest thou *Me?* Then love those who are *mine.* Thou knowest that it was said of Me ages ago: "*He shall gather the lambs in His arms and carry them in His bosom.*" Therefore, as the Good Shepherd, I have a special regard for the lambs. Feed them "*with the sincere milk of the Word, that they may grow thereby.*" Have a special care for the weak and tender ones. Look after the children and after such new disciples who are as yet *babes in Christ.* Labor for them. Feed them. Neglect not the older ones. Feed my sheep. Give to them who are able to bear it *the strong meat of God's*

Word. Let your whole life be a service in shepherding my flock. Thus let your love make you not only willing but eager to *spend and to be spent* in my service. Such service is a proof and a fruit of love. And without willingness to labor, professions of love amount to nothing. True love is something more than mere sentimental gush. Peter's love did thus prove itself. His whole afterlife was a service of love. How earnestly and enthusiastically he gathered in the sheep and the lambs! How glad he was to announce to that first in-gathered flock: "*For the promise is unto you and to your children.*" How eagerly he preached the Gospel in Jerusalem and Judea and Samaria, and afterwards was the first to carry it to the Gentiles, and thus admitted and tended some of the "*other sheep, not of this fold.*" He became second only to Paul in his missionary activity and left for the Church of all ages those two precious epistles addressed in general *to the strangers scattered abroad.* Peter's love bore rich fruit.

Finally, true love is ready to *sacrifice* and to *suffer*.

After Peter had so earnestly avowed his devotion to his Master, Jesus further told him that even confession in the face of opposers and blasphemers, and in addition to that a life of incessant and wearisome toil, was not all—that still severer tests would be made and still more precious fruit demanded.

"Verily, verily, I say unto thee, when thou wast young, thou girdedst thyself and walkedst whither thou wouldst: but when thou shalt be old, thou shalt stretch forth thy hands and another shall gird thee and carry thee whither thou wouldst not." Certainly very pregnant, earnest, and searching words! Words of the most vital import to all who would be or profess to be God's children! Jesus reminds Peter that there was a time when he was his own master. In those young days, when he knew not Jesus, he followed no law but inclination. *Thou girdedst thyself and walkedst whither thou wouldst.* What a lifelike portrayal of the unconverted youth! Such an one asks only, what do I feel like doing? Where do I feel like going? But now, Peter, thou hast another Master. Thou hast voluntarily become His follower. Thou professest to love Him. Now thou art no longer thine own. Now thou must always say, " Lord, what wilt *thou* have me to do? Henceforth *another* shall gird thee. All self inclination, all self pleasing, must now give way to pleasing Him who *first loved thee and gave Himself for thee.*

The time will come when because of thy love others will *carry thee whither thou wouldst not.* Peter had to suffer for his Lord before he could be glorified with Him. He was imprisoned. He was *girded* with chains to sentinel soldiers. He was bound to the whipping-post and scourged. And at last, as all the earliest records testify, he was bound to a cruel cross and crucified with his head downward. And thus, when he was old, he proved that his love was stronger than death, and by his death he glorified God. And thus did that love bear the final test and yield the choicest fruit. It was more than a sentiment.

Dear reader, Do you love Jesus? How is it with your *heart?* Is it listless, lifeless, cold? Or does it beat warm with affection? Does it yearn for closer and more intimate union and communion? Does it find delight in the communings of the closet? Does it bound with pleasure at sound of His Word? Does it find its highest joy in communing with that dear Master in His Church, in His Word, and especially His Sacramental Feast? Is that love of the heart ready whenever called upon to speak from your lips? When enemies surround you, when your Church, your Bible, your Lord are ridiculed and sneered at, are you ready always to defend them?. When you are questioned by the scoffer, when the finger of scorn is pointed at you, are you ready to say: "Yes, I am trying to be a Christian. I do love Jesus?"

Does your love prompt you to labor? Do you try to bring the straying and neglected lambs, the wandering and endangered sheep, into the fold of the Church? Do you try to feed them by telling them of Jesus and His love? How often have you spoken to your careless, God-less neighbor or acquaintance or companion about these things? How many unpleasant duties have you lately performed for Jesus? or how many disagreeable errands have you gone? *Lovest thou?* Feed! Feed! Feed!

Is your love willing to *sacrifice?* Do you still gird yourself and go where you feel like going? Or do you always ask yourself, Where does my Lord want me to go? What does He want me to do? Does your love always constrain you and permit Him to gird and lead?

And finally, Is your love willing to *suffer?* Are you ready, for love of Him who *loved you with an everlasting love, and with loving kindness drew you,* who stands before you with pierced hands and feet and side and asks, *Lovest thou me,* to meet opposition, to lose money, to lose friends, to cut associates, to turn your back on your former delights? Are you ready to take up your cross and follow Him?

Blessed are they who can look up and say and sing:

> "Do not I love Thee, O my Lord?
>   Behold my heart and see;
>   And cast each idol from its throne,
>   That dares to rival Thee.
>
> "Is not Thy Name melodious still
>   To mine attentive ear?
>   Doth not each pulse with pleasure thrill
>   My Saviour's voice to hear?
>
> "Hast Thou a lamb in all Thy flock
>   I would disdain to feed?
>   Hast Thou a foe before whose face
>   I fear Thy cause to plead?
>
> "Thou know'st I love Thee, dearest Lord;
>   But O, I long to soar
>   Far from the sphere of mortal joys,
>   That I may love Thee more.'

SERMON IX.

THE CONVERSION OF THE THREE THOUSAND.

ACTS ii. 37–42.

Acts ii. *37-42.* Now when they heard this, they were pricked in their heart, and said unto Peter and to the rest of the apostles, Men and brethren, what shall we do?

Then Peter said unto them, Repent, and be baptized every one of you in the name of Jesus Christ for the remission of sins, and ye shall receive the gift of the Holy Ghost.

For the promise is unto you, and to your children, and to all that are afar off, even as many as the Lord our God shall call.

And with many other words did he testify and exhort, saying, Save yourselves from this untoward generation.

Then they that gladly received his word were baptized: and the same day there were added unto them about three thousand souls.

And they continued steadfastly in the apostles' doctrine and fellowship, and in breaking of bread, and in prayers.

SERMON IX.

The scene of our text is laid in Jerusalem. The time is that memorable day of Pentecost when the Christian Church received her baptism from above, and was fully equipped for her work and mission. The church in Jerusalem was then made up of about one hundred and twenty members, with the twelve apostles for a nucleus. The apostles had been instructed by Jesus to *tarry at Jerusalem* until they would be *endowed with power from on high.* That full endowment had now come, especially upon the twelve, and also upon the whole one hundred and twenty; otherwise the prophecy quoted by Peter would not have been fulfilled. Not that there had been no Spirit upon the believers of the Old or New Testament before this. Had there been no Spirit of God at all, there could have been no believers at all. For the Grace that makes believers comes *not by might, nor by power, but by my Spirit, saith the Lord.*

But the Spirit had not come in His full New Covenant measure and power. This full and complete endowment of which the prophets and Christ had spoken, and for which all saints had waited and longed, had now come. The infant Church was now fully equipped and furnished for her great work. The endowment was to be permanent. The Spirit had come to stay. Jesus had promised Him as a substitute for His own visible presence. Jesus assured His sorrowing disciples that He would not leave them *comfortless* or *desolate* or *orphaned*. He had clearly and unequivocally promised, "*He shall abide with you forever.*"

Had He come as a transient visitor, to operate mightily and then depart, and at a time of special interest to come again, and thus arbitrarily come and go, and alight now on this one and now on that one, as some seem to imagine, the Church would indeed be left in an uncertain and comfortless state.

Since He came to stay, we need look for no more Pentecosts. The Spirit has been in the Church since that coming. Had He ever left the Church entirely, it would have ceased to exist. He began on that very day of His coming to operate through means. He did not fall on the three thousand as flames of fire, but reached them through Word and Sacrament.

It is the *Conversion of the Three Thousand* that we now desire to study.

We inquire *first* who were these three thousand?

It was the season of Pentecost. The city was crowded with strangers come from near and far to worship at the Feast. They were all Jews, or such as had accepted the Jewish religion. The blessings of the Gospel also were to come *to the Jew first* and then *through* the Jew to the Gentile.

Of these Jews, many were *devout*. They were sincere believers in and worshippers of Israel's God. To these belonged the persons who *were amazed and were in doubt, saying one to another, What meaneth this?*

Others were frivolous triflers or scoffers who *mocking said, These men are full of new wine.*

There were present also many who had been there at the last Passover. They had witnessed the exciting scenes of the trial and crucifixion of Jesus. They had joined in the insane cry of the multitude: "*Away with Him! Crucify Him! Crucify Him!*" Peter therefore directly charges them with having part in the awful crime of crucifying the Son of God.

All these people had now had six weeks' time for reflection. Some of them at least must have heard of the strange scenes that attended the death of Jesus. They had noticed the earthquake and darkness. They had heard of the rending of the temple's vail. They had heard also of the resurrection. The more thoughtful among them must have pondered and wondered and questioned concerning these things. To such a multitude Peter preached his sermon, and under it three thousand were converted.

We notice *secondly* the conversion itself.

In looking at the process of their conversion we notice how first *their minds were enlightened.*

They looked at and saw Jesus of Nazareth in an entirely new light. They saw that He was indeed the Anointed of the Father, the promised Messiah, the Son of God. They understood now that His coming, His life, His death, His resurrection, ascension, mediatorial reign and sending of the Spirit, that all this was a clear and complete fulfilment of the prophecies, the hopes, the prayers and longings of the saints of all ages.

On the other hand, they saw themselves in a new light. They were now willing to look deep down into their own hearts, and look back over their own lives. They saw their hearts full of nothing but sin. They saw their lives all defiled by transgression.

Thus were they enlightened to understand the

Saviour, His person and His work. Thus had they learned also to see themselves as poor lost and condemned creatures. This was the first step in their conversion. It ought to be the first step in every true conversion. Before we can expect any one to turn from the wrong to the right road, he must be instructed as to what is the right road, and why it is right, and conversely why the one he is on is wrong.

But enlightenment alone is not enough. It is not yet conversion. One might be considerably enlightened, and yet not saved. It is possible to have quite a clear understanding of Christ and His salvation, to know much *about* Him, and not *know Him* as a personal Saviour.

It is possible to have clear ideas of the nature and guilt of sin in general, to be able to give accurate and sound definitions of sin, to be able even to prove one's answers by properly quoted Scripture, and yet have no deliverance from sin and condemnation. The three thousand did not only have their *minds* enlightened; but *through* the mind the *heart* was reached.

This brings us to the *second* step in the process. *They were pricked in their hearts.*

Not only did they now know *about* Jesus of

Nazareth, and have entirely new views concerning Him, but they also *felt* themselves verily guilty because of Him. Not only did they see that in general all are sinners, and that sin in its inner essence is a rejection of Christ, but their own hearts were pierced with the awful feeling of their own fearful guilt and condemnation. They felt the awful load of personal guilt and ruin. Restless and self-condemned, each one was bowed low, and the language of his heart was: "*I abhor myself.*" Thus had the arrow of conviction pierced to the quick, and each one was ready to reproach himself as the guilty one. These were feelings of true penitence. This was that *godly sorrow that leadeth to repentance unto life, not to be repented of.*

And in such feeling we believe. More or less of it must enter into every true conversion. It came as the *result* of divine illumination. Instruction must come first. The mind must first be taught. The judgment must first be reached and influenced, and *through* it the heart or the feelings. The grievous mistake that many make, especially among modern revivalists, is that they appeal directly to and work immediately on the feelings. They play on the nerves, they work up an excitement, they rouse a deep and violent feeling, but it is of the flesh. It is not the result of intelligent conviction. Hence it is as the morning cloud and as the early dew. It is groundless enthusiasm, and results in the saddest disappointments and the most dangerous reaction, doubt, and often confirmed unbelief. Such feeling is not religion, but a snare and a delusion.

We notice in the *third* place how the three thousand had their *wills* influenced. Their desires and purposes were turned in a new direction. They manifested this in their anxious and sincere inquiry: "*Men and brethren, what shall we do?*" We have been doing wrong. We have been pursuing a sinful course. We now *want* to do right. We *want* to be helped on the right road.

Here was a true turning round, a real conversion. The language of the natural, sinful, and unchanged will is, "*we will not have this man to reign over us.*" The sad and repeated complaint of God and Christ is, ye *will* not come. I *would have* gathered thee. Ye *would not.*

These men now say *we will.* Only tell us *how.*

In every true conversion, as a result of an enlightened mind and a contrite heart there is a *changed will.* This was the *third* step. And now we see how the *whole* man was changed. There was a change in the intellect, in the sensibilities, and in the will. There were new views, new emotions, and new purposes. "*Behold, I make all things new!*"

In all this process we must also see the springing and budding of *faith*. Had they not believed what Peter preached unto them, they would not have been *pricked in their heart.* Had they not believed what Peter said about Jesus of Nazareth, they would not have felt guilty concerning their part in His death. Neither would they have accepted baptism in His name, and expected through it the remission of sins. They clearly believed. Their penitence had grown into faith. And thus we see that they had the elements of the new life, penitence and faith. And when Peter told them to *repent*, he here used that word in its broadest sense, as covering the whole process of conversion, and showing them that they were already "doing" what was necessary to salvation.

We inquire in the *third* place; "*How was this conversion brought about?*"

The answer is not far to seek. It was brought about clearly by Peter's *preaching of the Word.* Thus did God in the very outstart show to the young Church that henceforth His Spirit would operate *through* the Word, and that it *pleased Him by the foolishness of preaching to save them that believe.*

Peter, in preaching the Word, preached Christ as the very heart and substance of that Word. He showed them that this Pentecostal miracle was only a direct and clear fulfilment of their own prophecy; that their psalms also clearly predicted *Jesus of Nazareth, a man approved of God among you by miracles and wonders and signs, which God did by Him in the midst of you, as ye yourselves also know.* He went on to sketch rapidly the death, resurrection, and exaltation of this Jesus, and showed how David had foreseen and foretold all this. He charges them directly and plainly with the awful sin of rejecting and crucifying this Lord. He assures them that this same Jesus had *shed forth this which they did now see and hear.*

And this Word was the vehicle of the Spirit. Through it He convinced them of their own *sin*, their need of another's *righteousness*, even Christ's, and the certainty of *judgment* on all the children of the prince of this world. The Spirit of *wisdom* and *light* comes *through* the Word, and therefore "*The entrance of thy Word giveth light.*" The Spirit in the Word *convinced them* of sin, and therefore: "*By the law is the knowledge of sin.*" Their wills were turned, "*not by might nor by power, but by my Spirit, saith the Lord,*" and the Gospel, through which that Spirit comes, became "*the power of God unto salvation.*" They certainly did "not by their own reason or strength believe in Jesus Christ, their Lord, or come to Him," for "*No man can say that Jesus is the Lord, but by the Holy Ghost.*" That Holy Ghost came with the Word, and so "*faith came by hearing, and hearing by the Word of God.*"

They gladly received the Word. They might have resisted. This is man's melancholy prerogative. Man cannot take the first step towards saving himself. God must always come first to the sinner. But man can dismiss the Saviour when He does come. Man cannot raise himself out of the deep pit and the miry clay, but he can beat back the hand that reaches down from heaven to raise and save him. No doubt many who heard Peter did resist. The charge of Stephen a few weeks later was, "*Ye do always resist the Holy Ghost.*"

Thus does God reserve to Himself all the glory of saving man, and yet throw on man all the responsibility of being saved. It all becomes clear when we accept the old, sound and scriptural doctrine, that the Spirit of God carries the Grace of God *through* the *Word* of God.

But why did Peter instruct those people to be baptized? Was not the Word enough? Yes. And baptism is only another and a further application of that same Word, for "Baptism is not simply water, but it is the water comprehended in God's command, and connected with God's Word." (Luther's Catechism.) There is no valid baptism without the Word. Oceans of water, without God's Word used in the administration, would be utterly useless. Baptism has therefore been well called "the visible Word," or "the sacramental Word." There is a great blessing in baptism, *because* the Spirit-bearing Word is always connected with it. Therefore, these strong expressions, "*Born of water and of the Spirit;*" "*Be baptized .... for the remission of sins;*" "*The washing of regeneration and renewing of the Holy Ghost;*" "*Baptism doth also now save us;*" "*Baptized into Christ,*" and other like forcible passages.

There was indeed a great blessing to these penitent believers in their baptism. The preached Word carried the Spirit and Grace of God to them *collectively*. The sacramental Word carried them to them *individually*. The preached Word offered and carried forgiveness and salvation to the crowd. The sacramental Word carried them to them one by one. The former held out pardon and life to the mass, the latter to each one personally and individually, as if he were the only one. Under the preaching of the Word, some timid, doubting one might have said, "That is all very good, but I fear it is *not for me*." But when the water and Word of baptism are applied, and each one is taken singly and called by name, then faith is implanted and mightily strengthened, as each recipient realizes, the blessing is now bestowed on me personally.

And this individualizing, this taking of each penitent, hungry and thirsty one by himself, is indeed one of the chief blessings in both Sacraments, in the Sacrament of the altar as well as in the Sacrament of baptism.

And thus we see that the conversion of this multitude was brought about by the means of Grace, as ordained by Christ, the Great Head of the Church, viz., the Word and the Sacraments—for the other Sacrament also was used after they were baptized.

And these were indeed all the means that the apostles used at any time. They did not worry themselves with the question "How shall we reach the masses?" They had faith enough in Christ to believe in the means they had received from His hands, and these they prayerfully used.

And these same old means, wherever rightly used, have been effective in the conversion of sinners and the sanctifying of saints.

We might notice in passing here that these conversions, as nearly all the conversions recorded in the New Testament, were those of adults, to whom the Gospel had come *for the first time.* And *therefore* we read of *adult* baptisms. The parents had to be reached before the children. After the parents had become believers, we have no doubt whatever that they had their children also baptized. Peter, indeed, when he exhorts them to be baptized, says in the same breath, "*for the promise is unto you and to your children.*" As Jews also they knew that it was God's own order that infants had a place in the covenant, and received the Old Testament sacrament of circumcision. God had never revoked this, His own order of infant membership in His Church. Therefore it stood; for man cannot annul what God has ordained.

In conclusion, we notice briefly the evidences of these conversions.

First they were "*added*" to the apostles. In the last verse of the chapter it is said "and the Lord *added to the Church* daily such as should be saved." They at once became living and active members of the Church of Christ. A true convert always wants to have a spiritual home. He finds it in the Church. He cannot despise or make light of the institution founded by Christ for the salvation of man.

Again, they continued steadfastly in the apostles' *doctrine*. They accepted the teaching or doctrine of the apostles. They learned more and more of it. They held fast to it. They had no notions or opinions of their own. The *apostles*' doctrine was good enough for them. They wanted no faith except that which was *once delivered to the saints*.

Further: They continued in the *fellowship*, in the community, or brotherhood of the apostles. They wanted no other society. They no longer found pleasure in the company of unbelievers. They cut the acquaintance of those who were enemies of their Lord. A blessed fruit, a sure test of a true conversion. They *continued* in the fellowship.

And still more: They continued in the *breaking of bread*. That is, they ate their evening meals together. These meals were closed with the Lord's

Supper. They partook frequently and devoutly of that Holy Sacrament. No doubt they found it *meat indeed and drink indeed.*

A true convert always prizes highly the Communion of the Lord's Supper. He does not slight and neglect it for every trivial excuse. He finds in it the Holy of Holies of the militant Church, the most sacred spot and act this side of heaven.

And finally: They continued steadfastly *in prayers.* No doubt, they had their private prayers. There is no such thing as a Christian without prayer. While the true child of God wants to have his times and seasons to be alone with his Father, he also wants the help and blessing of public prayer. These early Christians wanted the prayers of the Church. They continued in prayer. Every believer wants the fellowship of prayer. He wants the Church's prayers. He wants to lift his heart upwards on the congregation's devotions. To him there is an inspiration and an elevation in such public worship, which lifts him above the sordid things of earth, and helps him to set his affections on things in heaven.

And thus did this new life of these new converts manifest itself. Thus did it develop and increase more and more.

Are we converted? Does our life thus manifest itself in the beauty of holiness, in the Communion of Saints?

> What strange perplexities arise,
> What anxious fears and jealousies!
> What crowds in doubtful light appear,
> How few, alas, approved and clear!
>
> And what am I? my soul, awake,
> And an impartial survey take.
> Does no dark sign, no ground of fear,
> In practice or in heart appear?
>
> What image does my spirit bear?
> Is Jesus formed and living there?
> Ah, do His lineaments divine
> In thought, and word, and action shine?
>
> Searcher of hearts, O search me still;
> The secrets of my soul reveal;
> My fears remove; let me appear
> To God and my own conscience clear!

SERMON X.

THE CONVERSION OF THE ETHIOPIAN EUNUCH.

Acts viii. 35-39.

Acts viii. 35-39. Then Philip opened his mouth, and began at the same Scripture and preached unto him Jesus.

And as they went on their way they came unto a certain water: and the eunuch said, See, here is water; what doth hinder me to be baptized?

And Philip said, If thou believest with all thy heart, thou mayest. And he answered and said, I believe that Jesus Christ is the Son of God.

And he commanded the chariot to stand still: and they went down both into the water, both Philip and the eunuch: and he baptized him. . . . . And he went on his way rejoicing.

SERMON X.

THE young Church had just received her first baptism of blood. Peter, who only a few weeks ago had shamefully backed down and denied his Lord because of the finger-point and sneer of a Jewish maiden, had now bravely suffered imprisonment and scourging, rather than cease *to teach and to preach Jesus Christ.* John, who had claimed that he was able to drink of his Master's cup, and be baptized with His baptism, not knowing what it meant, had shared with Peter in suffering imprisonment and the scourge. They had departed *from the presence of the council, rejoicing that they were counted worthy to suffer shame for His name.*

Stephen, the first Christian martyr, had died a cruel death, *for the testimony of Jesus.* And now the persecution had become general. A determined effort was made by those who had crucified the Lord to violently destroy His followers, and blot out that *new way which they called heresy.*

Then already, as ever after, "the blood of the martyrs was the seed of the Church." The Church multiplied rapidly in Jerusalem. The disciples also were forcibly scattered abroad in the regions round about. Wherever they went, they preached that same Jesus.

Philip, one of the seven deacons, who, like Stephen, was also an evangelist or public teacher, authorized and commissioned by the Church to preach the Word, had gone to the city of Samaria. There he had preached the Word with signal success, and multitudes were gathered into the Church.

True, the Church had already found that the Gospel net would gather in fishes, *both bad and good*, and that while they were sowing the *seeds of the kingdom*, an enemy was sowing *tares*, even *among the good wheat*. At Jerusalem Ananias and Sapphira had come in and had been excommunicated from above. At Samaria also, Simon the sorcerer had been added, on a false and hypocritical profession.

While Philip was doing a great work in Samaria, the Lord called him away from that seemingly important work, and directed him to go upon a lonely road in a desert country. Philip knew neither the destination nor object of his mission, yet he was not disobedient to the heavenly vision, but followed, *not knowing whither he went*.

Philip soon found that he was sent to preach

to an audience of *one* person. Quite a change from the multitudes who crowded to hear him in Samaria! Most of us would have said it was a serious mistake. But the Lord's ways are not our ways. He has a care for the individual. He sends His messengers after *one* soul. The ninety and nine must be left for a time, that the single wanderer may be sought and found. Would that all Gospel ministers and indeed all Christian priests or believers would recognize the opportunities and missions He gives them to preach Jesus *to the individual!* Then would the masses soon be reached.

Let us look at that individual for whom Philip must give up his great work in Samaria.

We find that as to *race* he was one of the despised of the earth. He was not of the chosen race, but by birth a Gentile. To him, therefore, did not pertain that birthright in the covenant and promises and oracles of God.

Worse than that, among the Gentiles he belonged to the most despised people. He was a descendant of the accursed Ham, an African from Ethiopia, a *negro.*

As to *position*, we do indeed find him among the great ones of the earth. He was treasurer of a great kingdom. He held the purse-strings of an empire, and had the dispensing of its silver and gold. In the eyes of men, his office would make him great and honored, in spite of his race. We will now consider *the conversion of this Ethiopian.*

As we find him already, to some extent, under the divine guidance, we naturally inquire *first:* What had the Grace that bringeth salvation already done for him?

We find that it had brought to him a knowledge of the true God. As we find him, he is not, like most of his countrymen, an idolater. He has learned to regard Jehovah, the God of Israel, as the only true God. This knowledge had probably been brought to him by some of the Jews, of whom there was quite a colony in Ethiopia at that time.

In accepting Israel's God as the only true Lord of Heaven and earth, he had to submit, as a matter of course, to the rite of circumcision. This made him a proselyte, and entitled him to a right to participate in the worship of the temple at Jerusalem.

We, therefore, find him an attendant of the great Feasts. We meet him on the way returning from Jerusalem, whither he had gone *to worship*. He had made the long journey from his own land in order to participate in the solemnities and festivities of Pentecost.

He had tarried in Jerusalem for several weeks after the Feast, and is now leisurely returning home. The fact that he was permitted to thus absent himself for so long a time, shows that he had the perfect confidence of his queen and her advisers. We, therefore, infer that he was, what Nathaniel was before he found Jesus, "*An Israelite in whom there was no guile.*"

It was now only about two months since the last eventful Passover. The memory of the tragic scenes of the crucifixion, and the stories of the resurrection, were still fresh in people's minds. The whole city had again been moved by the exciting scenes of Pentecost. Thousands of followers and believers had been added to the young Church. So confident and steadfast was the faith of these new converts that neither the dungeon, nor the whipping post, nor the prospect of death by stoning, could shake it or prevent its confession and promulgation.

All this the Ethiopian must have seen and heard at Jerusalem. In a devout and honest heart like his, all this would certainly awaken inquiries and longings for more light. This drove him to the Scriptures, and made him search anew the oracles of God. And thus we find that he was under the divine tuition. He was partially enlightened. He needed and was seeking further light. Prevenient Grace, the Grace that goes before and prepares the way for conversion, was at work in him.

We notice *secondly* how he was brought to the full light and life.

We find him reading the Scriptures. When he wanted more light and longed for more satisfaction, he did not try to satisfy himself by an effort of reason. He did not try to solve his perplexities with his own understanding. Neither did he say that he would wait until his return home, and then he would ask the philosophers and wise men of his own nation. It was not with any human light that he sought to dispel the darkness of his mind, nor with any earthly good that he endeavored to satisfy the longings of his heart. He went directly to the Word of God, believing that *the entrance of that Word giveth light*, that it is *a lamp unto the feet* and *a light unto one's path*. Looking up to the Author of that Word, his heart said, "*In thy light shall we see light.*"

He wanted the light of life. He went to the fountain of life. He found it in the book of life. These wonderful words of life were unto him *spirit and life*. Thus do we find this enquirer *searching* the *Scriptures* that in them he might *find* that *eternal life* which he craved.

We get a better idea of his eagerness and earnestness when we remember how inconvenient it was to read at that time. He was riding over a desert road, under the heat and glare of a Syrian sun. He was not riding in a palace car, but jolted along in one of the rude chariots of those days. Books and printing were not known. There were none of those handy editions of the Bible, nor vest-pocket Testaments. This man had to carry with him a heavy scroll of parchment, and this unwieldy roll of finely written manuscript he was trying to read as the chariot rumbled along. Truly he was interested. He could say, "*I have desired the words of thy mouth more than my necessary food.*" "*More to be desired are they than gold; yea, than much fine gold; sweeter also than honey and the honey-comb.*" He was seeking and finding light and life in the Word of God.

Further, we find this man gladly availing himself of the assistance of an evangelist. He did not belong to the class of those who are so *wise in their own conceits* that they imagine that they neither need nor could get assistance from others. Such are those people who say they need no ministers of the Gospel. They need not go to Church. They can just as well, or far better, read the Bible for themselves. They do not stop to inquire who instituted the office of the ministry. They do not try to inform themselves as to its origin, nature, necessity. Strange, that with all their professed Bible reading and Bible reverence, they have not found the ministry in it! Strange, indeed, that they could read the Bible without discovering that it is God's own ordainment that there should ever be these living teachers and preachers, because man needs the help of his fellow-man: and that the Lord, the great Head of the Church, has so arranged and ordered that His saving Grace, coming through the Word, should be brought *to* man *by* man. It is certainly clearly taught that God ordained the Old Testament priesthood, and that Christ appointed the New Testament ministry, and that, through the Church, which is His bride, He still calls and sends these preachers and dispensers of His written and sacramental Word.

So the eunuch believed. He humbly confessed that he could not understand all he read without some one to assist him. Finding one whom he believed to be a regular and true expounder of that Word, he appeals to him for instruction and light.

And Philip opened his mouth and *began at the same Scripture and preached unto him Jesus.* And thus did the living ministry expound and apply to him the living Word. The eunuch was preached to.

It is important to notice also the character of the preaching. It was true Gospel preaching. Not every-one who calls himself a minister or an evangelist is such indeed and in truth. There always have been *false prophets, blind leaders, and wolves in sheep's clothing.* They have come without being called of the Lord, they run without being sent.

Not all that is called Gospel preaching is such in reality. There be many who *preach another gospel, which is not another,* i. e., it is no gospel at all. Oh how many *preach themselves!* They stand before a congregation of poor, lost, and ruined sinners. Week after week they appear before them to display their own wisdom, to parade their own abilities, to magnify their own persons! How many preach *as pleasing men!* Their constant effort is to entertain, to flatter, to gratify the tastes and desires of the natural man! How much of the preaching of the present day is a magnifying of the innate powers and capabilities of man. An appeal to the pride and dignity of manhood, an effort to get man to lay aside vice *because* it is *unbecoming to such a noble and gifted creature.* Man's *manhood* is to *shame* him out of sin. Man's *pride* is to make him desire to be a son of God. Man's *noble endowments* are to be so developed that *by his own strength and reason he shall be as God!*

It was well for the eunuch that he did not meet some popular nineteenth-century preacher or evangelist!

Philip preached unto him Jesus. In this he showed himself to be a true evangelist. This is the substance of all true Gospel preaching. One greater than Philip had said, when urging the searching of the Scriptures, "*for they are they that testify of me.*" When preaching to a congregation of two, on the way to Emmaus, He began "*with Moses and all the prophets, and expounded unto them in all the Scriptures the things concerning Himself.*" Jesus was the burden of every Old Testament prayer, the hope of every patriarch and saint, the inspiration of every psalm, the aim of every sacrifice, the goal of every prophecy. *Jesus* is the very heart and life of the whole New Testament. *Jesus* was the great central theme, the sum and substance of all apostolic preaching and writing. Philip had a good text. He had a large subject. He had a theme that cannot be exhausted in one sermon, nor in the sermons of one lifetime, nor of all ages. It will take eternity to know and tell it all!

In preaching Jesus to this Ethiopian, Philip would naturally teach him the Bible doctrine of His *person* and His two-fold nature. He would unfold to him the great *work* or mission of Jesus, His life of obedience, the positive righteousness thereby wrought out—not for Himself, for He needed it not, but for those who were destitute of a righteousness that could stand before God. He would instruct him of the passive or suffering obedience of Jesus, even His *obedience unto death*, or His atonement.

Then he could not help explaining further what made all this great work of the God-man necessary. He would have to speak of *sin*, of its damnable nature and the necessity of punishment, and how that the work of Jesus was an expiation for man's sin, and that in it all He was the sinner's substitute. He would show that thus justice was satisfied, and redemption and salvation purchased for every sinner.

Again, it would be necessary to teach the Ethiopian how this *Jesus had sent the Holy Spirit*, and how that Spirit *applies* and brings home to the individual heart and life that redemption. He would show how that Spirit comes and operates through the Word and Sacraments, and how that Jesus had founded a Church in and by which the Word was to be preached and the two sacraments, Baptism and the Lord's Supper, administered. Thus would it be necessary for Philip in preaching Jesus to expound the way of salvation through Him, and the application of salvation, by His Spirit, through His Word and Sacraments.

That Philip did this becomes quite evident from the eunuch's request to be baptized. Whether the verse containing Philip's question and the Ethiopian's answer be genuine or not, even without it we find the clearest evidence of his faith. It was indeed because he believed so heartily in this Jesus Christ, that he believed confidently in all the words and institutions of Jesus. Such faith in Christ cannot make light of any of Christ's ordinances. Whether reason can see anything in the ordinance or not, faith believes that everything that comes from the hands of the Blessed One must, *on that account*, have blessing in it. Because the eunuch believed in Christ, therefore he believed in

Christ's baptism and wanted it applied to himself. It was not hard for him to believe "in one baptism for the remission of sins," and that "it worketh forgiveness of sins, delivers from death and the devil, and confers everlasting life and salvation on all who believe as the Word and promise of God declare." Believing in Christ, it was not hard to believe all that His Word says of the blessings and benefits of His sacrament. He wanted to be and was baptized. He wanted to have a place in Christ's Church.

Who will doubt his conversion? While there is not much said of his penitence or sorrow for sin, this is natural, because, as we saw above, he had been for a long time under the divine tuition. His faith, however, shines out brightly and clearly. Therefore, "*being justified by faith, he had peace with God, through our Lord Jesus Christ.*"

He went on his way rejoicing. He had found the *pearl of great price*, in comparison to which the treasures of Ethiopia were as nothing. He had found the forgiveness of sin and adoption into the family of God. He had found Christ in the Scriptures, and thus had the *key* to their interpretation.

This converted Ethiopian on his return to his native land would naturally tell *what the Lord had done for his soul.* He would naturally want to *teach transgressors God's ways, that sinners might be converted unto Him.*

Whether the early traditions that tell us of his turning evangelist and missionating among his countrymen are true or not, whether he did baptize his queen and establish the Church in that land or not, we cannot positively affirm.

But we do know that in the early centuries the Church seemed to find a ready footing and great prosperity in the north of Africa. And between that fact and the Ethiopian eunuch's conversion there may be a closer connection than we can trace. And if this be so, we need no longer wonder why the Lord directed Philip to leave his work in Samaria, to follow and evangelize one soul.

Who knows what results may follow the preaching of Jesus to a fellow-traveler, a companion, a neighbor, a fellow-workman, or an individual anywhere?

Let every Gospel minister and every member of the priesthood of believers do the work of an evangelist by preaching Jesus to the individual, whenever God gives the opportunity.

SERMON XI.

THE CONVERSION OF PAUL.

Acts ix. 1-9, and 17, 18.

Acts ix. *1-9, and 17, 18.* And Saul yet breathing out threatenings and slaughter against the disciples of the Lord, went unto the high priest,

And desired of him letters to Damascus to the synagogues, that if he found any of this way, whether they were men or women, he might bring them bound unto Jerusalem.

And as he journeyed, he came near Damascus: and suddenly there shined round about him a light from heaven.

And he fell to the earth, and heard a voice saying unto him: Saul, Saul, why persecutest thou me?

And he said, Who art thou, Lord? And the Lord said, I am Jesus whom thou persecutest; it is hard for thee to kick against the pricks.

And he, trembling and astonished, said: Lord, what wilt thou have me to do? And the Lord said unto him: Arise and go into the city, and it shall be told thee what thou must do.

And the men which journeyed with him stood speechless, hearing a voice, but seeing no man.

And Saul arose from the earth; and when his eyes were opened, he saw no man: but they led him by the hand, and brought him into Damascus.

And he was three days without sight, and neither did eat nor drink . . . . .

And Ananias went his way, and entered into the house; and putting his hands on him said: Brother Saul, the Lord, even Jesus, that appeared unto thee in the way as thou camest, hath sent me, that thou mightest receive thy sight, and be filled with the Holy Ghost.

And immediately there fell from his eyes as it had been scales: and he received sight forthwith, and arose and was baptized.

(Compare chapter xxii. 6-17, and xxvi. 13-16.)

SERMON XI.

It has been claimed that since the coming of Christ and the inauguration of the New Testament dispensation there has not been an individual conversion of such transcendant importance to the Church of Jesus Christ as the conversion of the apostle Paul. This claim may at first thought seem extravagant, but the more we study the life and character and achievements of that greatest of the apostles, the more are we inclined to accept the claim as sober truth.

Consider for a moment what kind of a man he was. He was endowed with one of the greatest and brightest of intellects. He had the advantage of a thorough and liberal education. He had been trained by the most reputable teachers, in the best of schools. His learning covered not only all the wisdom of the Hebrews, but it embraced also a thorough knowledge of the histories, the philosophies, the literature, and the mythology of the ancients of renown. As a scholar he probably had few peers and no superiors among his contemporaries.

He was a clear thinker, a strong reasoner, a powerful logician. Along with his bright intellect, he was possessed of a strong will, an indomitable purpose, a dauntless courage. With all this he had a scrupulous conscience and a tender heart.

Think of his former life and religious training. Brought up from childhood according to the tenets of "*the straitest sect of the Jews, a Hebrew of the Hebrews, a Pharisee of the Pharisees, as touching the law blameless.*"

With all the ardor and enthusiasm of his young nature, he had embraced what his famous teachers taught him as the old orthodox faith of the covenant people. He had become a thorough legalist and a firm believer in the coming of a world-conquering Messiah. All his associations, training and education had thus confirmed him more and more in what he considered as the faith of the fathers.

Now this educated and zealous man is brought face to face with *the new way*. He hears the preaching of the Galilean fishermen. They teach that one Jesus of Nazareth, a son of an obscure carpenter, whose pretensions had been rejected and condemned by chief priests, elders, scribes and Pharisees, who had died the disgraceful death of a malefactor, hanged between two thieves—that *this* was the Messiah, the Redeemer of the world! He is told that his own righteousness, which is of the law, and in which he prides himself so much, cannot save him; that he must repent as a poor sinner, and put his whole trust in the crucified Messiah.

No wonder that his whole being rises up in revolt at such doctrines and their teachers. He sees that the acceptance of this new faith means the overthrow of that colossal system of legalism and Messianic hope built up during centuries by Talmudists, Rabbis, Scribes and Pharisees. He eagerly disputes in the synagogues with Stephen and the other defenders of the new faith. He makes up his mind that this awful, revolutionizing heresy, this treason to Jehovah's covenant, must be exterminated root and branch. He becomes a leader in the persecution, takes part in the murder of Stephen, gives his voice or vote in the council against every believer in Jesus, lays hold of men and women, endeavors to compel them to blaspheme, and puts to death all persistent disciples. When through with his searching and torturing at Jerusalem, he starts to Damascus to carry on the same cruel work there. But before he gets there he becomes a believer in Jesus of Nazareth. He afterwards becomes the greatest of all the apostles, the most intrepid and invincible defender of the faith he once persecuted. Himself becomes the most persecuted man living. He endures such hardships, privations, tortures and torments, that his whole after life is a continuous martyrdom till it ends in a martyr's death. Surely such a man, *from* such a life, *to* such a life, could not have been converted *by* a delusion, *to* a delusion! No, to believe that would require far more credulity than to believe that he was converted by Him who is the Truth, to His own truth.

It is his conversion that we now desire to examine. Many false and dangerous errors have been drawn from and connected with this conversion. May the Spirit of truth lead us to know and accept His own truth.

We inquire *first:* What likely prepared the way for that conversion?

Whether Paul had ever been in Jerusalem when Jesus was in that city, we know not. But we do know that he was there a few years after the crucifixion, when the young Church was making such progress as to alarm the custodians and defenders of the old faith. He was there when there was that general interest and commotion caused by the preaching of the apostles and deacons. Paul must have heard some of that preaching and public reasoning in the synagogues.

It is also more than likely that he was one of those Cilicians who openly disputed or debated with the fiery and convincing Stephen. Unable *to resist the wisdom and the spirit by which he spoke*, they became wroth, and determined on physical force to put down the heresy. Paul, in the meantime, must have pondered and studied these new and wonderful truths. From the sincere and inquiring nature of the man, we believe that these wonderful words of life made him think, question, and feel. As long as he was unconvinced, he became the more hostile.

Stephen was dragged before the council, and made that masterly defense of his. Paul heard every word. It could not fail of an impression. It has been noticed how that, on more than one occasion, in his reasoning with the Jews, in later years, he adopted the same line of argument that Stephen used. He never lost that speech. No doubt it carried prevenient or preparatory Grace.

Then, again, as Paul listened to Stephen's convincing words, he also *saw his face as it had been the face of an angel.* With that look, reflecting the glory of heaven, he claimed, in Paul's hearing: *"Behold I see the heavens opened, and the Son of Man standing on the right hand of God."*

Paul heard that prayer for the murderers, and that peaceful committment of his spirit to the Lord Jesus.

With what feelings must not Paul have gone from that martyrdom! What a tumult must have raged in his breast! What conflicting thoughts and emotions must have stirred within! But he is not yet convinced. It is no trifle for a sincere, investigating, well-fortified, and perfectly satisfied spirit to throw off the convictions of a lifetime. Paul would likely blame his rising questions, doubts, and strange feelings on some unseen tempter. He would try to shake them off. He would drown them in redoubled zeal for the old faith. He would be more eager than ever to put down that new heresy, so subtle and dangerous as even to threaten to unsettle him! As long as he can find heretics, he keeps his head and hands full in Jerusalem. By and by he is through there. He cannot be idle. He must keep himself busy to keep down these troublous thoughts and feelings. Armed with the proper credentials, he starts for Damascus, to carry on the same awful, absorbing work there.

But Damascus is over one hundred and fifty miles away. It will take almost a week to make the journey. The route is over historic ground. The scenes along the way recall scenes and associations of great interest to the devout Jew. Along this way the impetuous and unsettled Paul must journey. He has nothing now to absorb his energy and attention. He is alone with himself. He has time to think. And such a man cannot dream away the time. *He must think.* The road would remind him of the covenant people and the covenant words. From these his mind would again revert to the new interpretation of those covenant deeds and words. Again and again he would recall the wonderful and elevating power of those new interpretations. Again and again the question would come, Is not the new interpretation more consistent and more true to the history and spirit of the covenant than the old? And then again would he feel the tortures of doubt and the indefinable longings after peace, and would send up a prayer to Abraham's God for light. And thus were those six quiet days, days of Grace and preparation. The Spirit of God was working through the Word and preparing the way for the Lord. The hammer was falling. The fire was burning. The light was shining. The seed was rooting; and Paul was in the way to conversion.

We therefore notice *secondly*, what brought that conversion to pass?

Paul and his attendants were nearing the city, *"And suddenly there shined around about him a light from heaven."* But it was not that light that converted him—it was only a symbol of another light that he needed, and that was about to be vouchsafed unto him.

In that light there appeared a form, and from that form there came a voice *saying unto him, Saul, Saul, why persecutest thou me?* It was Jesus revealing Himself and making Himself known through His own Word, and this brought about Paul's conversion.

Notice the *manner* of this revealing of Himself by Christ. He first *calls* him. He calls him by name. It is Christ coming first to Paul, and not Paul first turning to Christ. It is the shepherd seeking the sheep, and not the sheep the shepherd. Yes, God *always* comes first to us. The first step is from heaven to earth after the sinner, and not from earth towards heaven after God. That call is the call of seeking Grace. It is the call of yearning love. It is a repetition of that *first* call,

"*Adam, where art thou?*" It is the call that sounds so frequently in the ears of all of Adam's children.

Notice further how the Lord *enlightens* Paul. He shows him his sin. Thou persecutest *Me*. This is the awful character of sin. This is its damnable nature. It is opposition to Christ. It is rebellion against heaven. It is fighting against God. This is indeed the essence of all sin. Herein lies its fearful guilt. And this is what the sinner needs to know, and to know this he needs the light of God's Word.

The word of Christ shows Paul not only the guilt of his sin, but also its *folly*. It is a *kicking against the pricks*. As the stubborn ox only hurts himself by kicking against the sharp goad of the driver, so the sinner is only hurting himself. This is the folly of all sin. Even when it seems to give momentary satisfaction, it really brings sores and pains. It is a kicking into the sharp goad of Satan, the cruel driver.

The Lord further shows Paul the fearful *danger* of sin. As fighting against Jesus, to whom *all power is given both in heaven and on earth*, it is a hopeless battle. The sinner must miserably fail in the end. He will be utterly vanquished. He is only provoking *the wrath of the Lamb*, and laying up for himself *wrath against the day of wrath.*

Thus is Paul enlightened by the Divine Word. He is taught to see and understand what his sin is. Its nature, its guilt, its folly and its danger, are all shown him.

On the other hand, he is taught to know that there is One who loves him, who calls him, who is seeking to save him.

Now all this revelation of Christ is intended and calculated to awaken in Paul true *penitence*, a knowledge of sin, a sense of his guilt, and a longing for deliverance. And this is the first part of conversion.

Christ's interest and call is also intended and suited to beget *faith* in Paul. It is calculated to draw him to that compassionate Seeker, and to enable him to cast himself on His mercy. Faith is to come *by hearing, and hearing by the Word of God.* But faith is the second part of conversion.

That such was the result with Paul we can plainly see from his conduct. Paul *fell to the earth;* but that fall was not conversion, it was only a symbol of that coming down of his sinful pride, self-sufficiency and self-righteousness.

We find that the prostrate and humbled Paul

first *inquires* for more light. "*Who art thou, Lord?*" Paul has become an inquirer. He wants to be certain first of all with whom he has to do. It is a blessed token of a work of Grace when the sinner begins seriously to inquire about Christ and divine things, when he goes to his Bible to find out who this Lord is and what he desires of him, and what he himself is over against this Lord. Paul further asks: "*What wilt thou have me to do?*" It is a further cry for light and instruction.

But this question is also more than that. It contains an acknowledgment of sin. What wilt *thou* have me to do? As much as to say: "I have been following my own way. I have been doing my own works. My way, I now see, is all wrong. It is *the way of Cain*, the way of death. My works have been works of darkness and crime against my Lord. I acknowledge my transgression. I hate my sin. I abhor myself." Such we believe were the penitent feelings of the contrite heart of Paul.

This question of Paul also contains a confession of faith in Christ. "I acknowledge Thee to be my *Lord*, only do *Thou* direct; I will trust Thee; I will put myself in Thy hands; I will follow Thee. No longer will I consult my own inclination or my own reason. Thou shalt direct and Thou wilt save." And thus the turning point was made. Paul was a converted man. But he was by no means a full-grown man in Christ Jesus. He was but just *a babe in Christ*—a feeble beginner of the Christian life. We notice, therefore, *thirdly:*

The further leadings of Divine Grace towards the fuller light of assurance and the higher calling of apostleship.

Paul was blind. That light above the noon-day brightness of the Syrian sun had temporarily darkened his eyes. He was led by the hand into the city. For three days he sat in the gloom and saw no man. This doubtless was to further teach him how dark his way had been without *the Light of the world.* During these days *he did neither eat nor drink.* He was as one who had been hanging over a fearful gulf, and was suddenly rescued by a heavenly hand. He could not help but review the past, reflect on his awful course, lament over his fearful sins, shudder at the frightful danger that he had been inviting, and cry again and again for mercy, even after he had obtained mercy. The only account we have of the occupation of these momentous days is, "behold, he prayeth." What pleading and wrestling that must have been! Then he was further instructed by one commissioned to be a spiritual guide. From Ananias he learned the way of God more plainly. He brought to that broken and contrite heart the heavenly light, and life, and comfort of the divine Word. As a new-born babe he desired and received *the sincere milk of the Word, that he might grow thereby.* Ananias also instructed him to receive the Sacramental Word, that *"washing of regeneration and renewing of the Holy Ghost,"* which *"doth also now save us." "And now why tarriest thou? Arise, and be baptized, and wash away thy sins, calling on the name of the Lord."*

And thus, by the Word, as he had studied it before his conversion, as he had heard it from Stephen, as he heard it from Christ and from Ananias, as he received it in connection with the baptismal water, was Paul led out into the blessed light of acceptance, into the family of the redeemed, and the full assurance of forgiveness and inheritance among the saints in light.

It is a general opinion that Paul at once, as soon as he was baptized, entered upon his public ministry. If we had no other account of his conversion and mission than the Acts of the Apostles, then such would be our natural conviction. But Paul gives us many details in his letters, which are not mentioned in the Acts. In the first chapter of Galatians, after speaking of his former life and how it pleased God to call him and reveal His Son in him, he says, "*Immediately I conferred not with flesh and blood; neither went I up to Jerusalem to them which were apostles before me; but I went into Arabia, and returned again to Damascus.*"

Comparing this statement with the account in Acts, it seems that, after his baptism, Paul spoke a few times in the synagogue of Damascus, thus professing publicly his new faith, and that then he retired to Arabia, where he was alone with his Lord, in training for his great work for a part of three years. Thus, like Moses in Midian, and afterwards in the mount, like Elijah in the desert, and Christ in the wilderness, like Luther in the monastery, and afterwards in the Wartburg, Paul was first schooled and prepared for his arduous mission. Only after that did he enter fully on his apostolic labors.

In closing, let us still notice briefly what was extraordinary and miraculous about this conversion, and what was ordinary. The extraordinary features were the blinding flash of light, the vision of the glorified Christ, and His audible personal address to Paul, as also his prostration and blindness. These extraordinary manifestations and experiences need not be expected to be repeated. To wait and hope for such things, is to expect that for which there is neither ground nor promise. They were clearly exceptional, and no one has a right to look for their repetition. Whoever puts off his conversion in hope of some such manifestations, will probably die unconverted. Neither were these extraordinary features the real agencies of Paul's conversion. They were only the incidental and attending circumstances. The real means of the conversion were its ordinary features.

These were, on God's part, *the Word*. Through it Christ revealed Himself and His seeking Grace. Through it He convinced Paul of his sin. Through the spoken and sacramental Word brought by Ananias, Paul received and was assured of the forgiveness of sin.

On the part of Paul the ordinary experiences, as a result of the operation of the Word, were the sense of sin or penitence and faith.

Such are the ordinary means of Grace, and such Grace comes still through such means, and such converting power they still carry. These are the ordinary features of Paul's conversion. They are its vital and essential elements. They are repeated with varied experiences and phenomena in all conversions. They can be had by every sinner. They are herewith offered to every unconverted reader of these pages.

SERMON XII.

THE CONVERSION OF CORNELIUS.

ACTS x. 1–6.

Acts x. *1–6.* There was a certain man of Cesarea called Cornelius, a centurion of the band called the Italian band.

A devout man, and one that feared God with all his house, which gave much alms to the people and prayed to God always.

He saw in a vision, evidently about the ninth hour of the day, an angel of God coming in to him, and saying unto him, Cornelius.

And when he looked on him he was afraid, and said: What is it, Lord? And he said unto him, Thy prayers and thine alms are come up for a memorial before God.

And now send men to Joppa, and call for one Simon, whose surname is Peter:

He lodgeth with one Simon, a tanner, whose house is by the sea-side: he shall tell thee what thou oughtest to do.

SERMON XII.

The very interesting chapter from which our text is taken, records the conversion and reception into the Christian Church of the first Gentiles. No doubt there had been Gentile converts received into the Apostolic Church before Cornelius. But they had all become converts to Judaism first. They had come into the Christian Church through the door of the Jewish. They had first submitted to circumcision and all the ceremonial requirements of the Law of Moses. Thus they had become proselytes of righteousness and worshippers in the temple of Jerusalem.

Cornelius and his household were uncircumcised, and were not attendants on the temple services. Without these hitherto essential requirements, they were admitted to full membership in the infant Church. This was the turning of a new leaf in the Church's experience and polity. It was a radically new departure, an epoch of the most vital and far-reaching consequences.

It is interesting to notice the characters that figure in this most important transaction.

The apostle who was commissioned to bring

about the conversion and admittance into the Church of these first Gentiles was Peter.

Now, as far as we know, there was scarcely another apostle so intensely devoted to the traditions and ceremonies of the Fathers as he. It required a vision, thrice repeated, a special message from heaven, and a plain and distinct commission from the Spirit, to remove his prejudices and doubts and make him willing to go to Cornelius.

It is also of interest to study the history and character of the first Gentile convert. This will appear as we now consider more particularly the conversion of Cornelius.

We notice *first:* His unfavorable surroundings.

It is said that man is a creature of circumstances. Much is said and written of the potent influence of environment. And while environment is wrongly made the excuse for many sins of omission and of commission, yet we must admit that it is a factor in the shaping of life and character.

Some persons are so situated that it is almost a matter of course that they should take an interest in religion. Others, however, are so circumstanced that everything seems to be against their taking an interest in spiritual things.

Not that we believe these things a valid excuse

for the neglect of salvation. Where there is the proper earnestness and interest one can find Christ and be true to Him in any honest and honorable calling and amid the most adverse surroundings. Joseph maintained his integrity in Potiphar's house and at Pharaoh's court. Obadiah remained true to his God at the corrupt court of Ahab and Jezebel. And Daniel did not defile himself, but devoutly worshipped and obeyed his God, even in Babylon.

Cornelius also was begirt with unfavorable surroundings. By birth he was a heathen. He had no birth-right in Israel, and was not of the chosen race. He was born an alien to the covenant, a stranger to the commonwealth, and excluded from their promises. He belonged to that idolatrous nation whose corruption and degradation are so vividly portrayed in the first chapter of Romans. At the time when godlessness, abomination, and crime of every kind had reached their flood-tide in the empire, Cornelius held a government office. We know to our sorrow that even in Christian lands comparatively few government officials pay much attention to religion. What then could we expect from an officer of the Roman Empire in its darkest days?

But, worse than that, Cornelius was a soldier, an

army officer, centurion, or captain, of the Italian band or company. Military life has always been looked upon as unfavorable to earnestness in religion. Soldiers even in Christian lands are noted for God-lessness, looseness of morals and general recklessness. The camp, the field, and the march seem to have a withering influence on everything that is spiritual. Now Cornelius was a captain in Cæsar's army. Surely his calling and situation were not calculated to make him a devout and earnest inquirer after the true God and the right worship. His environment was against him. From a human standpoint he would not be considered a very hopeful subject for conversion. And yet, in spite of all this, he was an exceptionally good man.

Let us notice therefore, *secondly*, his good character.

He was a strictly *honest* man. His servants, who ought to know him, bring this report to Peter: *Cornelius is a just man and of good report among all the nation of the Jews.* The Jews were certainly not partial to the Roman soldiers. They were far more ready to see the sins than the virtues of these their enemies.

If a Roman centurion therefore had a good report among the Jews, his character must have been of exceptional uprightness. In attributing to him such a character for honesty, the Jews and the servants of Cornelius agree.

But honesty is not religion. A man can be scrupulously just and upright in all his dealings, and yet be and remain a stranger to God and His Grace. Honesty alone can never save the soul. On the other hand, however, let it never be forgotten, that while honesty is not religion, yet there can be no true religion without honesty. There never can be saving Grace in the heart and wilful dishonesty in the life. A man may talk ever so earnestly about his experience, he may pray ever so fervently in prayer-meeting, if he does not make every effort to pay his honest debts, if he cheats in his business transactions, takes advantage of ignorance, adulterates his goods, gives short weight or measure, misrepresents value, or does dishonest work, we take no stock in his piety. To be a Christian one must be honest, but one can be honest and not a Christian.

Cornelius was also a *liberal* man. *He gave much alms to the people.* It is a good thing to be liberal. To be large-hearted and open-handed is certainly no small virtue. But liberality in itself is not religion. A person can give liberally and freely to every good cause, even while he has an unregenerate heart. There are many who have no saving interest in Christ who yet give largely to Christ's poor and to Christ's Church.

Again, however, we must also bear in mind that while one can be liberal without being in a state of Grace, one cannot be in a state of Grace without being ready to communicate. We have no faith in a stingy Christian. According to the divine Word *covetousness is idolatry*. He who professes to love Christ and is yet unwilling to give to the cause of Christ, loves only in word. If it hurts him to give instead of giving him joy, if he complains when asked to give back a part of what God has just lent him, instead of rejoicing that he is able to give, there is something seriously wrong with his heart. A true conversion reaches the pocket-book as well as the heart. Grace enlarges the heart and opens the hand.

So while Cornelius had the virtue of liberality, this would not necessarily prove him in a state of Grace. But he was, further, a *devout* man. *He feared God with all his house, and prayed to God always.*

It is possible to be a devout heathen. Those who were loyal to the divinities of Rome and their temples and shrines, those who regularly brought their sacrifices and offerings, were devout worshippers of false gods. It was not in this sense that Cornelius was devout. He had long since seen the folly and sin of recognizing and worshipping the myriad gods of Rome. He had learned to recognize Jehovah, the God of Israel, as the one and only true God. It was Jehovah that he feared. It was Jehovah that he taught his family and servants to fear. It was to Jehovah that he prayed *always*, i. e., habitually and regularly.

In this also Cornelius was in advance of many who profess to be children of God and members of the Church of Christ. It is a humiliating fact that there are thousands of professing Christians who seldom if ever pray. They allow the pastor to do the praying for them. They know not what it is to bow the knee in the closet and pour out the heart and heart-yearnings before God. Much less do they pray with their families. Their children grow up around them without an example of either private or family devotion. And as to praying with their servants and encouraging them to pray, this would seem to them preposterous. The servants are treated as if they had no souls. There are no provisions for their spiritual wants. They are almost compelled to live heathen lives in socalled Christian families. Cornelius prayed. He prayed with his family. He prayed with his servants.

Then he was certainly a child of Grace, a converted man, a true believer! Was he? Not necessarily. It is indeed possible to have a correct knowledge of the true God, to offer Him an outward worship, and even to have regular habits of prayer, and yet not be a subject of His saving Grace. There is certainly no healthy Christian life without prayer. Prayer has been aptly called the pulse of the new life. And yet one can have the form of prayer without its spirit and life. Not that we think the prayers of Cornelius hypocritical, engaged in for the express purpose of deceiving. Neither were they altogether lifeless and formal. But they were not yet the outbreathings of a renewed heart. We believe that Cornelius was seeking after more light, feeling after God, if haply he might find Him, as a wandering child finds a loving father, and nestles in his strong arms.

This leads us to inquire *thirdly*, What did Cornelius still want?

We know that there are those who contend that he was already a true believer, or a converted man.

After a careful study of the whole subject, we are persuaded that he was in the way towards conversion, was being prepared for it by his study of the Word, his prayers, and strivings. But the *one thing needful* he had not yet found.

If Cornelius had been already in the way of salvation, why was he directed to send for Peter? And why did Peter consent to go? The servants who came for Peter remained with him a part of a day and a whole night. Peter had ample time to inquire into the character and attainments of Cornelius. Why, after hearing such a good report of his character, his good works, and his devotion, did Peter still consent to go? Why not dismiss these servants, with the message to Cornelius that he needed no further light or Grace? Evidently Peter did not believe that Cornelius was already in a state of Grace.

This becomes still more manifest when we read in the fourteenth verse of the eleventh chapter that the angel told Cornelius that he "*shall tell thee words whereby thou and all thy house shall be saved.*" If he needed words whereby he *should be saved*, he was not yet in the way of salvation.

Again, in the eighteenth verse of the same chapter, after Peter had rehearsed the whole story to the doubting brethren, we read: "*When they heard these things they held their peace and glorified God, saying, Then hath God also to the Gentiles granted repentance unto life.*" Cornelius therefore had still needed that *repentance unto life.*

It would seem then that he still needed a clear idea of the sinfulness of sin, a realizing sense of his own guiltiness, his need and helplessness. He needed to learn that sin was such a serious, death-bringing and damning thing, that his own good works and devotions could not render satisfaction and make him acceptable in God's sight. True, God was well pleased with his searchings and strivings and efforts. But all these could not save him. He needed a change of heart, a repentance unto life. He was too much of a poor, lost and condemned creature to bring this about by his own strength or reason. He needed "words" to bring him to such repentance, and to save him. These *words* were not only to inform him about sin and about one *mighty to save*, but they were to bring this Saviour to him, and him to this Saviour. For "*to Him give all the prophets witness that through His name, whosoever believeth in Him shall receive remission of sin.*" Cornelius needed to give up all confidence in self, and to put his whole trust in a crucified Redeemer. Only after this had taken place could it be said that he had passed from death unto life.

We notice *finally* how this change was brought about in Cornelius.

The change that he needed could be brought about "*not by might nor by power*, (*i. e.*, not by human might or power,) *but by my Spirit, saith the Lord.*" He needed that Spirit to convince him of his own *sin*, of his need of another's *righteousness*, and of a *judgment to come* on all those who are not delivered from the *prince of this world*. In other words, he needed the Spirit of God to bring him to repentance and to beget faith in him.

And how did he receive that Spirit? Jesus had said, "the words that I speak unto you, *they are spirit and they are life.*" And that this applied not only to the words that fell from His own lips, but to the preaching of all who would preach His Word, becomes clear when we remember how He breathed on His apostles, and said, "*receive ye the Holy Ghost,*" and afterwards: "*He that heareth you heareth me . . and he that despiseth you despiseth me.*" The whole Word of God is therefore called an *administration* of the Spirit, and *the sword of the Spirit.* In the former sermons on the conversions of the New Testament, we have seen how the Spirit of God every time brought the renewing Grace of God *through* the Word of God. So here Peter was to bring *words*, mere words. And what good could words do? By them or through them Cornelius was *to be saved*. Peter brought words; He preached, He preached Christ, His coming, His office, His work, His death, His resurrection, and His return to judgment. He preached the necessity of Faith in this Christ, and the certainty of the remission of sins through faith in His name. These words were *spirit and life*. They carried the Spirit, and therefore this preaching of the Gospel was *the power of God unto salvation* to Cornelius also. It pleased God *by the foolishness of preaching to save* Cornelius and his household.

While Peter preached *words*, the spirit fell *visibly* on those who heard. He does not always come thus visibly. He ordinarily comes invisibly but effectually through the Word. But this was a special case. It was the first coming of the Spirit of Pentecost to the uncircumcised. Apostles and believing Jews did not believe that the Spirit would come upon the uncircumcised. In order to fully convince Peter, in order to convince the six Jewish witnesses who had come from Joppa with

Peter, in order to remove every possible doubt from the minds of the Gentiles themselves, therefore, He came in this instance visibly. Therefore He came not as usually through the preached and sacramental Word, which was afterwards administered. It was thus for special reasons that He separated Himself on this occasion from the Word while it was being preached, and fell in visible form.

We see then how Cornelius was saved by the *words* preached, followed by the sacramental Word of baptism.

But the Word had to be *preached*. It had to be preached by one called of God. This also is God's order. It has so pleased Him that His saving Word should be brought to man by man. The angel might have preached to Cornelius. He might have brought to him the words that he needed. But this is not God's plan. If the Ninevites are to be warned, Jonah must needs go and preach the preaching that he is commanded. If Saul of Tarsus asks, "*Lord, what wilt thou have me to do?*" the Lord does not tell him, but directs him to go and wait for one Ananias. And if Cornelius sees an angel and asks him: *What is it, Lord?* he is directed to send for Peter. And so it is still. The ministerial office is a *divine* institution. As such it is necessary, but let no man take this office unto himself *but he that is called, as was Aaron.*

And thus was Cornelius converted.

This whole history is of the most vital importance to the whole Church of Christ. It teaches that one can go quite far in professions, in works, and in worship, and still be in an unsaved condition.

If such a good man, and of such good report, and honored for his devoutness, if such an one still needed conversion, how is it with us? What of our hearts? Do we know what penitence is? —what trusting, clinging faith in Christ is? Do we experimentally *know Christ and the fellowship of His suffering and the power of His resurrection? Examine yourselves, whether ye be in the faith: prove your own selves.*

SERMON XIII.

THE CONVERSION OF SERGIUS PAULUS.
Acts xiii. 6–12.

Acts xiii. *6–12*. And when they had gone through the isle unto Paphos, they found a certain sorcerer, a false prophet, a Jew, whose name was Bar-jesus:

Which was with the deputy of the country, Sergius Paulus, a prudent man; who called for Barnabas and Saul, and desired to hear the word of God.

But Elymas the sorcerer (for so is his name by interpretation) withstood them, seeking to turn away the deputy from the faith.

Then Saul, (who also is called Paul,) filled with the Holy Ghost, set his eyes on him,

And said, O full of all subtilty and all mischief, thou child of the devil, thou enemy of all righteousness, wilt thou not cease to pervert the right ways of the Lord?

And now, behold, the hand of the Lord is upon thee, and thou shalt be blind, not seeing the sun for a season. And immediately there fell on him a mist and a darkness, and he went about seeking some to lead him by the hand.

Then the deputy, when he saw what was done, believed, being astonished at the doctrine of the Lord.

SERMON XIII.

THE apostle Paul was just starting on his first missionary journey. Of his labors from the time of his conversion up to this point, we have only the most general account. He had labored some in Damascus, in Jerusalem, in his native city of Tarsus, and in Antioch. In the latter city he and Barnabas had labored for about a year, and gathered quite a congregation. It was there also that *the disciples were first called Christians.*

It was not the mission of the great apostle, however, to be the settled pastor of a congregation. He had been called to the more important and difficult work of a traveling missionary. It was to be his work to be a pioneer, to go ahead, preach the Gospel in places where it had not yet been heard, gather congregations and plant Churches in these new places. He was not to enter upon other men's labors, but was rather to lay foundations for others to build on.

It was while Barnabas and Paul were busy at Antioch, and while their work was prospering abundantly, that the Holy Ghost said to the

Church: *Separate me Barnabas and Saul for the work whereunto I have called them.* Departing from Antioch they had sailed to the island of Cyprus. There they preached first in the city of Salamis, and from thence they went to the western end of the island, to the city of Paphos. Here also they entered vigorously upon their work of preaching the Gospel. But here, as everywhere, they found that the devil had been there ahead of them. So it has always been, and so it is to-day. The prince of this world gets in his work first. We are indeed all born under the dominion of sin and Satan. Every human heart, in its natural state, is the abode of sin, and where sin is there is Satan also. And therefore every city and country and clime are more or less under his dark and mysterious sway. Wherever missionaries go, at home or abroad, into churchless districts or Christless homes, they find that the devil has been there before them. They find that he will oppose every effort they make to bring in the kingdom of God and establish *the right ways of the Lord.* The prince of darkness had a special and powerful emissary in the capital city of Paphos. Through his wicked agent he tried, as he always does, to bring the governor of the island completely under his sway. He is crafty enough to know that if he can get a ruler, a king, a mayor, or any one of authority and influence, it is a mighty help to his cause.

The two missionaries had to meet him. It came to an open contest. The result was the conversion of Sergius Paulus, the first prominent conversion under Paul of which we have any account. We consider this a very important conversion. Some conversions are more important than others. Not that one soul is of more value in God's sight than another. *He is no respecter of persons.* In his sight the soul of Sergius Paulus, the governor of Cyprus, is of no more value than the soul of one of his slaves. Both are equally the purchase of the precious blood of Christ. Still, the conversion of Paulus is of greater importance and of greater value to the Church, because of his position, his authority and influence. He could do more for the young Church and new faith than one of his slaves, and therefore we consider his an important conversion.

In studying this conversion, we inquire *first* into the history, character and position of the man.

Sergius Paulus was a Roman, and therefore a heathen. He had been bred and brought up in the state religion of the Roman empire. That religion was at that time the most vile, corrupt, and criminal heathenism on the face of the earth. We have a graphic picture of it in the first chapter of Romans. Sergius Paulus had, from childhood up, drunk in its abominations and criminalities. Surely all this was against him.

But, notwithstanding all this, we read that he was *a prudent man.* He was a thoughtful man, given to sober investigation and clear discernment. This is all the more to his credit, when we recall the fact that, in those dissolute times, there were few men who were prudent thinkers. It was a time when most Romans of means and leisure were wholly given up to the indulgence of the lusts of the flesh. To revel in dissipation, debauchery and vice was the chief occupation of Roman citizens. This was especially true of government officials. Their position seemed to entitle them to *'rioting and drunkenness, and chambering and wantonness.* And to these they gave their attention, their money and their time.

Sergius Paulus was Proconsul, or governor of Cyprus. As a quiet and peaceful province, this island was under the control and patronage of the Senate. As such it required very little governing, and the office of Sergius was without much care or responsibility. It would have been the most natural thing therefore for him to while away the tedium of his monotonous life by headlong indulgence of the flesh. Add to this the fact that the capital city Paphos was the reputed birthplace of the goddess Venus, and that her impure worship flourished abundantly there. Consider the influence on public life and morals which that most unchaste of all idolatries would have. Then remember that to all this temptation Sergius Paulus was exposed. And still he remained a *prudent* man. This speaks much for his intelligent and moral character.

Such was Sergius Paulus, the governor of Cyprus.

Let us notice *secondly* his deeper longings.

He evidently believed in the higher powers of an unseen realm. He was convinced of the existence of beings and influences beyond and above the regions of sense. He had faith in the supernatural. As a serious, reflecting and candid man, he felt that this earth is not the only abode of man, and this life is not the whole of existence. He realized that man is related to two worlds. No doubt his conceptions were very vague, and his ideas very crude. How could it be otherwise, when his only guides were nature, conscience and the ignorant pretenders of a degraded religion? The belief in the unseen powers of an unseen world is inborn with man. He can only rid himself of it by a positive and persistent effort of his will. Indeed, it is doubtful whether man ever really gets rid of this innate conviction. It is more than likely that all thoughtful skeptics are like that one in Ohio, who said: "I do not believe in a hereafter, and yet I would give my best yoke of oxen *if I were sure* that there is none." The conviction is too deep-seated to be easily got rid of, and however individuals may here and there try to become atheists, the mass of mankind must always believe in some kind of a god, and in some kind of a religion. So it was with Sergius Paulus. He had no doubt accepted the religion of the Empire in his earlier days, but he had become disgusted with and discarded it. It had degenerated into such open and public fraud and knavery, that its own priests scarcely believed in it. Cicero tells us that in his day two priests, while ministering together in the temples of the gods, could not look each other in the face without laughing.

But Sergius Paulus was not ready to throw away

all religion. He felt that somewhere there must be a true religion; one that could satisfy the cravings of the heart. Would that all who have been deluded by the vagaries of man, as if these were the revelation of God, would thus seek for the truth until they find it, and the peace which it alone can give.

Sergius had heard of the Jewish religion. Its purer and sterner faith had attracted many thoughtful strangers, who became proselytes. Now there was a Jewish sorcerer or magician in Paphos. He doubtless passed himself off as a representative of the Jewish faith. Sergius Paulus had heard of his pretensions to occult powers and mysteries. He had sent for him with the hope of finding that truth and satisfaction.for which he longed. This deceiver was present at the governor's court when the two missionaries of the Gospel began their work in the city. Sergius Paulus heard of their preaching of the Gospel of the Son of God. He heard how they claimed to be the ambassadors of Jehovah, the God of Israel, and to bring His message; how they preached that Jesus of Nazareth was the Redeemer and Saviour of mankind, and had been delivered up to the cross for man's offences, and raised again for his justification, and that whosoever believeth in Him should have the full and free remission of all his sins. The simple and earnest preaching of these sincere and devoted missionaries had made an impression in the city. The governor had heard about it. The tricks and pretensions of his magicians had failed to satisfy him. The rumors of the evangelists and their pure and wondrous message had waked in his heart also longings after the pure and holy. *He called for Barnabas and Saul, and desired to hear the Word of God.* This desire for the Word shows the workings of preparatory Grace in his heart. It was an important step towards his conversion when he sent for these preachers of the Gospel.

It is always a very hopeful and helpful step, when the sinner, weary of the vagaries and speculations of men, seeks out the true ministers of the truth, and desires from them light from the Word of God. Or, uncertain to whom to go,' if he resorts simply to his Bible, and prayerfully seeks the light from its sacred pages, such an inquirer is already entering upon the way of salvation.

We notice *thirdly* the work of the Word with Sergius Paulus.

The Word was preached to the governor. It was preached in all its plainness and with all its power.

It was a new revelation to Sergius Paulus. Such wonderful words of life he had never heard. The Word was making way in his heart, and he felt himself convinced, convicted and drawn.

The sorcerer saw that he was in danger of losing his profitable and influential position. Satan does not give up his votaries and victims without an effort to hold them. The governor was too valuable an adherent to give up. He must be held at all hazards. The Word of God is not allowed to have free course. It must be mightily opposed. Barnabas and Saul must be refuted or silenced. "*Elymas the sorcerer withstood them, seeking to turn away the deputy from the faith.*"

So it always is. The proverb says: "Where the Lord builds a church the devil puts up a chapel along side of it." There are not wanting those who like this sorcerer oppose the Word, and try to turn every prospective convert away from the faith.

We have then the ambassador of Christ and the child of the devil face to face. We have on the one side the plain unvarnished Gospel, on the other all *subtilty* and *mischief* and *perversion*. We have open candor in conflict with knavery, treachery and lies. The prudent governor looks on. He hears both sides. He sees the truth and error face to face. Like Jannes and Jambres who withstood Moses and Aaron in the presence of the ruler of Egypt, so Elymas withstands Paul in the presence of the ruler of Cyprus. What will the outcome be? Pharaoh had hardened his heart and sided with the magicians, against Moses and Aaron.

But Sergius Paulus does not harden his heart. He does not resist the truth. He does not stifle conviction, or grieve the Spirit, or dismiss Paul as another ruler afterwards did, and said: *"Go thy way for this time; when I have a more convenient season I will call for thee."* The mind of Sergius is unbiased. His heart is opened. He hears and receives the truth. The truth comes out triumphant. Truth needs never to be afraid of error. Truth is mighty and must prevail. Wherever hearts are not barred against it, truth does prevail. All it asks is an unprejudiced mind and a sincere heart.

Sergius saw and felt the superiority of the truth. He saw the trickster and liar confounded. He saw the righteous indignation of Paul against the impostor. He heard the authoritative and stern rebuke of villainy. He saw its power. He saw the would-be miracle worker stricken blind.

In the stern rebuke of the sorcerer, Sergius must

have felt himself rebuked for harboring such a *child of the devil and enemy of all righteousness.* This must have moved the governor to shame and contrition. Otherwise it would have moved him to anger. He felt the rebuke, he bowed under it. He repented of his sin. He cherished that *godly sorrow that leadeth to repentance not to be repented of.*

Further, he *believed*, as a prudent, clear-headed, and wise man. He weighed the truth. He was convinced of its superiority. So is every candid inquirer. He felt its power in his own heart. He saw its power on the wilful impostor. He was astonished *at the doctrine.* He accepted the doctrine because he saw and felt its power. Why don't unbelievers now judge the doctrine by its fruits? Why will they shut their eyes against its effects? Why deny its purifying and transforming power in those who sincerely accept it? Why deny its conquests over error and opposition? Sergius saw the power and was astonished at the *doctrine. He believed.*

He was therefore a converted man. He had true faith, and true faith presupposes penitence. And penitence and faith make up conversion.

We see again how the Spirit wrought *through*

the Word. The Word, as the organ of the Spirit, did the whole work. The Word is the Lord's agency in every conversion. There can be no true conversion without the Word. There are true conversions wherever hearts bow to the power of the Word.

Does any one read these pages who has not found peace in believing? Reader, are you such an one? You believe in another life and another world. You have felt your need of some kind of a religion. You have perhaps made trial of something that has called itself the religion of Jesus Christ. You have been deluded, disappointed. Have you then thrown away *all* religion? Why not follow the example of Paulus? Go to the Word of God. It will satisfy. It will save. It has never disappointed an honest seeker after truth and life. It will not disappoint you.

SERMON XIV.

THE CONVERSION OF LYDIA.

ACTS xvi. 13-16.

Acts xvi. *13–16*. And on the Sabbath we went out of the city by a river-side, where prayer was wont to be made; and we sat down, and spake unto the women which resorted thither.

And a certain woman named Lydia, a seller of purple, of the city of Thyatira, which worshipped God, heard us:

Whose heart the Lord opened, that she attended unto the things which were spoken of Paul.

And when she was baptized, and her household, she besought us, saying, If ye have judged me to be faithful to the Lord, come into my house, and abide there. And she constrained us.

SERMON XIV.

THE Apostle Paul was on his second great missionary journey. Before he started out on this memorable tour, and during the early part of its progress, he had met with several sore disappointments, so that his plans and purposes seemed to be repeatedly thwarted. It was while making preparations to start out from Antioch, that he had that unhappy quarrel with Barnabas, which separated these two pioneer missionaries in their future activity. In Galatia, it seems, the Apostle was detained by a long and severe sickness. When they wanted to go into the province called Asia, they *were forbidden of the Holy Ghost to preach the Word there.*

Again, *when they assayed to go into Bithynia, the Spirit suffered them not.*

Thus Paul might have said like Jacob of old, *All these things are against me.* And yet how clearly all was overruled for good. Even in that unhappy strife God made *the wrath of man to praise Him.* Instead of one missionary band starting out there were two, and instead of two missionaries there were four. It was during these disappointments also that Paul found and became acquainted with young Timothy, who became his most constant friend and helper and his greatest comfort. It was during the providential detention in Galatia that he gathered the Churches in that wild region. And had it not been for that we would probably not have had that important and instructive epistle to the Galatians. But most wonderful and best of all were the hindrances and refusals to work in Asia and Bithynia. That work was to be done by others. Paul had a more important present mission. Therefore came that remarkable vision and that sad, impressive cry from that man of Macedonia.

What a cry that was! It came from a people that had tasted world empire, and had been left unsatisfied. It was a translation into words of that remarkable scene, when, four hundred years earlier, Alexander had returned from conquering the world, and sat down on the seashore and wept like a child because there were no other worlds to conquer, and his heart longings were not satisfied. That Macedonian cry! It came from a people that had enjoyed the civilization, and culture, and art, and science of Greece in her palmiest days. It came from a people that was now enjoying the splendor, and renown, and law, and order, and indulgence of Rome. And still that people cried for *help!* They asked it of a poor and obscure preacher of the despised religion of the cross! What a cry was that, from such a people to such a helper! Oh yes, it is the same cry that has sounded down the ages. We hear its echoes in the corridors of the centuries. It is borne across the waters, and from the western prairies, and ranches, and mining camps to-day. It is the old cry from the world to the Church. It is the sad wail that comes from the tenement districts, from alleys and courts, from the abodes of sin and suffering in garret and cellar, from every Christless home and heart. *Come and help us!* We cannot help ourselves. The world cannot help us. Its money, its friendships and flatteries, its pleasures and indulgences, cannot still these longings. We need what the Church alone can bring. We need the living Gospel of a living Redeemer. Without that Gospel in the home and in the heart,

> "What am I but a child crying in the night,
> What am I but a child crying for a light."

Paul and his companions were not disobedient to the heavenly vision. They hastened across the gulf. They assuredly gathered that the Lord had called them to carry the Gospel *into Europe*. They went to the important city of Philippi. For several days Paul, and Silas, and Timothy, and Luke, walked up and down in that strange city. They found very few Jews. There was not even a synagogue. The people seemed not even to know that there was a God of heaven and earth. The missionaries found no place or opportunity to begin their work. They learned that there was a place of prayer by the river-side, just outside of the city, where a few devout persons were in the habit of meeting on the Sabbath day. Thither the four missionaries went. They found a few women, some Jews, and some proselytes. What a congregation! What a place to begin missionary work in Europe! But the missionaries did not despise the day of small things. They *sat down and spake unto the women*. They preached to them as Jesus preached to the woman at Jacob's well. And that was the first preaching of the Gospel in Europe. Its immediate result was what we will now consider:

THE CONVERSION OF LYDIA.

We consider *first*, what she was before her conversion:

By nationality she was not a Jewess. She was *of the city of Thyatira*. This city was in the Roman province of Asia, in which these missionaries were forbidden to preach. Ancient historians inform us that the inhabitants of the district about Thyatira were so corrupt in their manners that the fact had become proverbial.

In this place and among these people Lydia had been born and brought up.

As she was by birth a Gentile, she was, as a matter of course, an idolatress in religion. From her childhood she had been trained in the abominations and superstitions of heathenism.

By occupation she was a merchantess, *a seller of purple*. There was a guild of dyers, an association of merchants, such as we would call a union, or a trust, in Thyatira, whose goods were much sought after everywhere. Lydia was probably a member of this guild, and had a branch or an agency at Philippi.

As to her circumstances, Lydia was what in those days would be called rich. She had a house in Philippi that was large enough to accommodate the four missionaries in addition to her household. She had means enough to entertain these men comfortably while they were in the city, and she doubtless was one of those Philippians whose liberality afterwards helped to support Paul in his old age and imprisonment, and also ministered to the poor saints at Jerusalem.

Now all these things were certainly not calculated to predispose her to give serious attention to religion. They were rather all hindrances to a pious disposition. Her Gentile birth and heathen training were against her. Her occupation would tend to fill her more and more with the cares of this life, and make her more and more worldly. The deceitfulness of riches would exert its withering influence on her and make it hard to enter the kingdom of God.

And yet, in spite of all this unfavorable environment, Lydia had made certain advances towards a better life. Instead of demoralizing more and more, she had improved herself. She had renounced heathenism. She had learned about Jehovah, the God of Israel, the Maker of heaven and earth. She had accepted the teachings concerning the true God. As far as she knew Him, she believed in and worshipped Him. It was in such a state and condition that Paul found her.

We inquire *secondly*, What did she do towards her own conversion?

From what we are told further on about her heart being *opened*, it is clear that her heart was originally *closed* against divine Grace. And this is indeed the sad truth as to every heart so long as it is in its natural and unrenewed state. The unregenerate heart is "*deceitful above all things and desperately wicked.*" Out of it proceed "*evil thoughts, murders, adulteries, fornications, thefts, false witness, blasphemies.*" "*Every imagination of the thoughts of man's heart is only evil continually.*" The natural man has his "*understanding darkened,*" "*is alienated from the life of God through the ignorance that is in him, because of the blindness of his heart.*" He "*receiveth not the things of the Spirit of God . . . . neither can he know them,*" He is "*in darkness,*" "*dead in trespasses and sins.*" His heart is a "*heart of stone.*"

It is of course utterly out of the question that the sinner should by his own reason or strength be able to change a heart so wicked, corrupt, blind, stony, dead. If that heart is to be opened, changed and quickened, it will certainly be not by human "*might nor by power, but by my Spirit, saith the Lord*," for "*no man can say that Jesus is the Lord, but by the Holy Ghost.*"

And yet Lydia did something towards her conversion.

What did she do?

First, she heard the Word. She had heard it from the Jews. Through it she had learned the sin of idolatry, and the doctrine of the true God. She attended the public worship of the believers in the true God. She went to church with them. She associated herself with them in their worship and hearing of the Word. Secondly, she entered heartily into that worship. *She* worshipped. She was not a disinterested looker on. She prayed herself as best she could. Thirdly, when Paul came and spoke the New Testament Word, the sweet and precious Gospel of Jesus Christ, she *attended* unto the things which were spoken of Paul. She gave attention; she listened eagerly; she lost not a word; she took it all in.

Thus much the sinner can do. He can seek out and associate with God's people. He can go with them to church. He can hear the Word of God. He can hear that Word attentively, and when that Word stirs up longings, he can express them, even if in inarticulate, halting and broken petitions. This is his part in the work. Thus much did Lydia do towards her conversion.

We inquire *thirdly*, what did God do in her conversion?

The simple words of the record are, "*whose heart the Lord opened.*"

We have seen certain seeds encased in such close and hard pods that one would wonder how they would ever open. But in the gentle rains of early autumn those pods would become soaked, as little by little the moisture worked its way in, until gradually they would spread, and the seams would open and let the full drops fall on the seeds within.

We have seen the rose-bud hanging on its stem enfolded tightly in its green casings. But as the sunshine would fall upon that bud, as its gentle warmth would work its way inward, reaching fold after fold, the shriveled leaves would unfold and spread until the outer casement was broken, and by and by the full blown rose in all its queenly beauty drank in the full rays of the sun, and gave out its rich and odorous perfume. And thus was the heart of Lydia opened.

How did the Lord open it? Through His Word. That Word of which He says: "*As the rain cometh down and the snow from heaven, and returneth not thither, but watereth the earth and maketh it bring forth and bud, that it may give seed to the sower and bread to the eater, so shall my Word be that goeth forth out of my mouth: It shall not return unto me void; but it shall accomplish that which I please, and it shall prosper in the thing whereto I sent it.*" Again He says: "*My doctrine shall drop as the rain, my speech shall distil as the dew, as the small rain upon the tender herb, and as the showers upon the grass.*" Thus had the Lord opened her heart through the Word. Through it the *sun of righteousness* did rise upon her *with healing on His wings.*

That Word had come to her first as the law. She had learned first from the Old Testament, of which the law was best known and first taught to proselytes. Through this the prevenient or preparatory Grace of God had reached her heart. This law taught her to see, and made her feel, her need. It awakened and intensified in her a longing for salvation. The law became her *schoolmaster to bring her to Christ*—*i. e.*, her leader to take her by the hand and lead her towards Christ.

And now when this preparatory work had been softening and making ready the heart, Paul brought the life-giving Gospel. And through this *power of God unto salvation* the Lord more fully opened her heart. This Gospel not only showed her and instructed her about that Jesus who shall *save His people from their sins;* but this Gospel brought that very Saviour home to her heart. *"Say not in thine heart, who shall ascend into heaven, that is to bring Christ down from above, or who shall descend into the deep, that is to bring Christ up again from the dead."* For *"the Word is nigh thee . . . that is the Word of faith which we preach."* Thus Christ comes through the written and preached Word, through it He opens the heart and enables the sinner to open it, as He says: *"Behold, I stand at the door and knock; if any man hear my voice and open the door, I will come in to him.* It is by *hearing His voice* as it sounds in His Word, that He opens in such a way that in one sense the sinner opens, with the strength that comes in hearing.

But Christ also comes through the sacramental or visible Word. *"Know ye not that as many of you as were baptized into Jesus Christ were baptized into His death?"* *"For as many of you as have been baptized into Christ have put on Christ."* This sacramental Word concerning which Paul, who everywhere speaks of it in such strong terms as a positive bearer of Grace, must have instructed her in his discourse, Lydia also desired. Paul administered to her then and there this Divine means of Grace. Through it her heart was still more fully opened, and Christ was brought more fully into that heart; and thus Lydia was converted.

We might here refer to the question in passing, Why are the individual baptisms mentioned in the New Testament all those of adults, and why is there no distinct and specific mention of infant baptisms? Waiving here the question of the four family baptisms that we have recorded, besides four others that we can legitimately infer, we answer as follows: First. The labors of the apostles were *missionary* labors, and not the labors of settled pastors in well established congregations. As missionaries, they had to begin with the parents and adults. When these were converted they were baptized, and if parents, their households. The same procedure is necessarily followed by our missionaries at the present day. Their first baptisms are adult baptisms. They would not baptize the children while under the control of heathen or unbelieving parents. It would be as legitimate to infer and try to prove that our missionaries do not believe in infant baptism because they report annually so many adult baptisms, as to conclude that the apostles disbelieved in infant baptism because we have the record of their adult baptisms. Secondly. And this is an important point. Even if we should grant—as we by no means do—that there is no account of infant baptisms in the Bible, where is there a single instance of the baptism of an adult *who had grown up in a Christian household?* Such an instance would be parallel to the adult baptisms in the Baptist church of to-day. But there is none. Every single adult baptism mentioned is that of a *convert* from Judaism or heathenism. *Such* adult baptism we also practice. But why is there no instance of the baptism of one grown up in a believing family? It was more than thirty years from the death of Christ to the death of Paul—plenty of time for the children of his first converts to become adults. Were they baptized? When? The record tells us that when parents were converted and baptized, their *households* were baptized. Bengel pertinently asks: "Who can believe that in so many families there was no infant? And that the Jews who were wont to circumcise, and the Gentiles who purified them by washings, did not also present them for baptism?" No, no; the idea of excluding children from the covenant blessings is contradictory to the whole scheme of redemption and to the inmost spirit of the Gospel. God Himself ordained infant membership in His church. He alone has the right to revoke it. He has never done so, therefore it stands. Infants had a place in the old covenant. The new is not narrower but wider. The promise was to Lydia and to her children, if she had any. Her household was baptized.

We notice briefly in conclusion, The Fruits of Lydia's Conversion. The first fair fruit of that change of heart, was a change in her home. It became henceforth only really worthy of that sacred name, *home*. A Christian home is a type of heaven. Outside of a sanctuary of the Most High, there is no spot on earth more happy, holy and heavenly, than a Christian home. There is a "*church in the house*." There the religion of the blessed Saviour permeates the whole atmosphere. There the Word of God dwells richly. There are altars of prayer, and closets for prayer. There Jesus is a daily and well-known Guest. There the children, baptized into Christ, are nourished with the sincere milk of the Word, and grow thereby. In such a home, parents and children, all children of one Father, kneel at one altar, with the same trust, the same love, the same hope, the same Lord.

The religion that God ordained in the old covenant was essentially a *family* religion. The religion of the new covenant is the same. Where father or mother are converted, one of the fruits of that conversion is a change in the home life. Such was one of the fruits of Lydia's conversion.

Another fruit of that conversion was that she at once began to cultivate a true Christian hospitality. This also was a New Testament fruit from an Old Testament seed. Hospitality was practiced by the patriarchs and saints of old. They were not forgetful to entertain strangers, and thereby some had entertained angels unawares. This Christian grace Lydia now cultivated.

Luke, one of the four missionaries, writes: "*She besought us, saying, If ye have judged me to be faithful to the Lord, come into my house and abide there. And she constrained us.*" She took in the four missionaries. She entertained and provided for them while they were in the city. She freely, of her substance, ministered to their necessities.

And what a gain it must have been to her! She furnished the missionaries a home and meat and drink. They gave to her the bread and water of life, and thus nourished her for life eternal in the heavenly home. Thus was she further instructed and strengthened in the new life. Thus was she more and more sanctified through the truth of God's Word.

And this was the beginning of the evangelization of Europe. Here is encouragement for missionaries and ministers. Here is inspiration for laborers in new and hard fields. Here is hope for small congregations. Let ministers be faithful like Paul, let converts be true and devoted like Lydia, and the Word will grow and multiply.

SERMON XV.

THE CONVERSION OF THE PHILIPPIAN JAILOR.

Acts xvi. 25-34.

Acts xvi. *25-34*. And at midnight Paul and Silas prayed, and sang praises unto God: and the prisoners heard them.

And suddenly there was a great earthquake, so that the foundations of the prison were shaken: and immediately all the doors were opened, and every one's bands were loosed.

And the keeper of the prison awaking out of his sleep, and seeing the prison doors open, he drew out his sword, and would have killed himself, supposing that the prisoners had been fled.

But Paul cried with a loud voice, saying, Do thyself no harm: for we are all here.

Then he called for a light, and sprang in, and came trembling, and fell down before Paul and Silas,

And brought them out, and said, Sirs, what must I do to be saved?

And they said, Believe on the Lord Jesus Christ, and thou shalt be saved, and thy house.

And they spake unto him the Word of the Lord, and to all that were in his house.

And he took them the same hour of the night, and washed their stripes; and was baptized, he and all his, straightway.

And when he had brought them into his house, he set meat before them, and rejoiced, believing in God with all his house.

SERMON XV.

AFTER the Gospel had gained its first foot-hold in Europe through Paul's speaking the Word to a few devout women, gathered for prayer at the river side, just outside of Philippi, the house of Lydia, the first European convert, became the headquarters of the new cause. Paul and Silas and Timothy and Luke made that house their home during their stay in the city. For many days they prosecuted their work with peace and prosperity. They still preached to and prayed with the people who met at that river side.

But trouble soon arose. The kingdom of God cannot be built without opposition from the kingdom of darkness. The prince of this world would not stand idly by and see the Gospel gain a permanent footing in Europe. His ingenuity and power must be employed to kill this new life in its beginning. The devil uses many and various means. He is fertile in resources. He is cunning, crafty and full of guile.

At Paphos he had withstood and fought against

Paul openly. Paul had met, resisted and routed him. At Philippi he tries a new plan. He had failed to frighten as a roaring lion. He will now flatter as an angel of light.

For many days a certain damsel possessed with a spirit of divination, *i. e.*, an evil spirit by which she charmed, told fortunes and astounded the people, followed the apostles. In the hearing of the people who gathered to hear the apostles, she continually uttered this remarkable cry: "*These men are the servants of the most high God, which show unto us the way of salvation!*" Noble words! Blessed testimony!

But why should an evil spirit utter such sentiments? It may have been from constraint. The evil spirit may have recognized in that Christ, whom these servants of the most high God preached, their Master and Judge. Like the demoniac of our Saviour's time, who cried out in terror before Him, and confessed Him to be the Christ the Son of the Living God, and acknowledged that He would one day torment them as their judge; so the evil spirit in this poor maiden may have cried out and confessed in terror.

But it may also be that this evil spirit offered the Apostles his help and co-operation. It may be that it was his dark design to help along the preachers, to preach the Gospel himself, in order to draw them into a league with himself, and afterwards easily overthrow their whole work. No doubt he has in this way beguiled and ruined many a Gospel minister and many a congregation.

But, whatever may have been the motive of that cry, Paul would no more accept testimony to the truth or any kind of help from the devil, than would Christ his Master. "*Paul, being grieved, turned and said to the spirit, I command thee, in the name of Jesus Christ, to come out of her. And he came out the same hour.*"

Now this damsel was a slave girl. She was the property of her masters. They had been making money out of her soothsaying and divining. They *saw that the hope of their gains was gone.* They loudly and vehemently accused the Apostles before the magistrates as law-breakers and disturbers of the public peace. Pretending to act in the interest of law and order, they inflamed the multitude and the magistrates against the preachers. Mob law was invoked. Without trial or sentence the Apostles were scourged, thrown into the inner prison or dungeon, their feet fastened in the stocks, a kind of a foot-rack, forcing the feet apart and holding them in a vise-like grip. And thus with bruised and bleeding flesh, quivering with pain, without light or air, or food or drink, were the sufferers left for the night. What a night was before them! Little did they know that it was to be a night of triumph and conquest for them. And yet, so it turned out. It witnessed *the jailor's conversion.*

In studying that remarkable conversion, we look *first* at the jailor himself, and his environment.

We know little about him as a man. Of his former life we know nothing. We only know that he was a heathen in that corrupt and cruel age.

His office was a menial one. Even now it is the exception to find a refined and humane person occupying the position of jailor.

But prison life and rule is vastly different from what it was in the dark days of heathenism. The religion of Jesus Christ has thrown its softening, sympathizing, and refining influences even into the gloom and degradation of prison life. There is still much room for improvement. Christian principles do not always prevail in so-called Christian cities. There is too much heathenism in too many hearts and lives. But, with all this, it is vastly better than it was. And even where Christian principles are professedly disbelieved, their influence makes itself felt.

In the days of Rome's declining glory, as a rule, the low, corrupt and heartless were selected as jailors. Even if upright and humane before, the exercise of their office would tend to degrade them. They worked and lived with the vile and abandoned. Day by day they would see scenes of degradation and brutality. They were compelled to hear profanity and vulgarity. They would be exasperated by the conduct of those under their care. They were compelled to be inhuman and cruel. If not naturally without feeling and hardhearted, they would perforce become more and more so. To this class the Philippian belonged. Such were his occupation and associations. Surely all these things were against him.

His environment gave little promise of a better life. He would be considered a rather hopeless subject on which to expend missionary effort. It is not the least of the glories of the young Church that she won so many of her converts from the ranks of those who seemed to be in every way predisposed to wickedness and unbelief. It is no small testimony to the power of the Gospel that it can and in every age does reach, convert, and entirely change the hearts and lives of such persons.

We desire to notice *secondly*, that conversion itself. In studying this it is well to notice what preceded it and likely prepared the way. We recall the significant cry of the possessed damsel: *"These men are the servants of the most high God, which show unto us the way of salvation."* This cry had been publicly uttered for many days, by one notorious in the city. Quite naturally it became the talk of the town. The jailor also would hear about it. Questions would be asked, "Who is that *most high God?*" "What is that *salvation*, and what that *way* which these strange messengers proclaim?"

Paul had, by a word in the name of Him whom they preached, driven out the spirit. The girl had become quiet and rational. What did it all mean?

The principal preachers of this new way of salvation had been rudely and illegally arrested, dragged before the city magistrates, condemned without a trial, stripped of their clothing and cruelly beaten with rods. Under all this abuse and torture it seems that the victims uttered no word of complaint or malediction.

Faint and bruised and bleeding, they were given into the custody of the jailor, who, it seems, witnessed the whole violent procedure. He was charged to keep them safely. When he violently *thrust* them into the inner prison and made their feet fast in the cruel stocks, they did not curse him, as he probably expected. Their whole demeanor must have impressed him deeply. He had never handled such prisoners before.

Leaving them thus in their misery and agony, the jailor went to bed. Now, if the man had any thought and feeling at all, what would be more natural than that he should lie down thinking of these strange men, their strange conduct and their strange work in the city? And so he went to sleep with strange and new thoughts and feelings. And in that sleep, perchance a restless, dreamy sleep, what dreams he may have had! Judging from the sequel, we believe that prevenient Grace was at work. He was being prepared for conversion. In a tragic and dramatic way was that conversion brought to a crisis.

The two notable prisoners meanwhile were sitting and suffering through the weary hours. And how did they beguile away the long tedium of the night? "*At midnight Paul and Silas prayed and sang praises unto God.*" The prisoners heard them. Never before, we opine, had such sounds been heard in that place. Those cells and corridors were wont to resound with curses and maledictions. If ever the voice of song had been heard there, it must have been the maudlin mutterings of the ribald wretch. And now the music that rises and swells through those sad and gloomy cells, at that midnight hour, is a song of prayer and praise to the most high God.

And while their God is giving to these martyrs *songs in the night*, another strange event occurs, no doubt as an answer to those midnight prayers and praises. The foundations of the old prison begin to tremble and the walls begin to rock. So violent becomes the earthquake that the chains are loosed from the prisoners, the stocks fly from their feet, and the doors stand wide open! Did they stop singing? We believe not. Why should they, when they recognized heaven's amen to their devotions?

The jailor is startled from his fitful slumbers. He springs up frightened and almost frenzied. If the singing is still going on, he neither hears nor heeds. He sees the open doors. He believes the prisoners are fled. He knows his life will have to answer for their escape. Roman-like, he decides on suicide. He draws his sword—but is arrested.

Paul sees or hears what is going on. He calls out in a clear tone, "*Do thyself no harm.*" How much is in these words! They proclaim the whole aim and object of the Gospel. It is the intent and purpose of this blessed Gospel of the Son of God to keep mankind from self-inflicted harm and ruin. He who is harmed and ruined is so by his own hand. Whoever perishes under the sound or in reach of the Gospel, is a spiritual suicide.

"*We are all here.*" We, servants of the most high God, would not fly, because we are under our God's protection, and fear not what man may do unto us. The other prisoners heard our prayers and praises. They see the answer. They desire to remain with us. The language of their hearts is "*Thy God shall be my God.*" And so we are all here. The jailor saw the influence and power of these servants of the most high God.

And now he recalled again that momentous cry of the sooth-saying damsel. What did she say? Who are these men? "Servants of the most high God." And how were they treated? And how did they bear it? They did neither abuse nor curse me. Didn't I hear them singing? And they keep all these prisoners here, though the doors are wide open. Oh yes! They must be messengers of the Most High. And what am I over against these men? How have I ill-treated them? How have they suffered at my hands? What a wretch I am! Their God sent this earthquake. He will take vengeance on me. Whither shall I fly? But hold! What did that girl say? "*They show unto us the way of salvation.*" Is there a way to be saved? Would that I knew it. I'll ask them: "*Sirs, what must I do to be saved?*" I am lost. I want to be saved, if I only knew how. Tell me. What must I do? I'll do anything.

Thus, we judge, was conviction doing its work in his heart. Paul answered that anxious and momentous question. How brief his answer! And yet how full! Does it not contain the very marrow of the Gospel? What is the theme and import of the Gospel? Is it not this? Man is a poor lost and condemned sinner. Jesus Christ came into the world to save sinners. He offers Himself through His Word and sacraments. Wherever thus offered, the one great fundamental, all-conditioning and damning sin, is *unbelief.* The one underlying, all-conditioning condition of being saved is *faith in Christ.* And all this is embraced in Paul's answer. And then Paul goes on and speaks to him and his whole household *the Word of the Lord.*

He thus leads that now *turning* inquirer on into the full light of trust and assurance. Taking his own brief answer to the jailor for a text, he would naturally go on and instruct him further. He would instruct him about the Lord Jesus Christ, His coming, His person and work. He would explain the benefits that flow from that atoning work. He would show how the Holy Spirit applies those benefits through the Word and Sacraments. How that by these repentance is wrought, faith begotten, and Grace imparted. Thus would he show to the inquirers *the way of salvation.* In pointing out the way, he would be leading the hearers into that way. In learning *about* Christ, the Word would enable those who rightly heard, to *know Christ and the fellowship of His suffering, and the power of His resurrection.* And here indeed is one of the chief glories of the Word of God. It not only tells *about* salvation, but in its words *it is able to save* the soul.

Paul believed strongly in the Sacraments. He had such implicit faith in Christ, that he had faith in everything that comes from the hands of Christ.

In his writings he lays great store by baptism, and calls it "*the washing of regeneration, and renewing of the Holy Ghost.*"

He would naturally instruct the jailor and his household as to the nature and benefits of this holy sacrament. They accepted the instruction. "*He was baptized, he and his, straightway.*"

And thus was the jailor converted. In his conversion we can clearly trace the two component elements, penitence and faith. His trepidation, prostration and anxious cry show a deep-felt abhorrence of self and sin. His desire to be saved implies a confession of being lost and being helpless. His penitence was deep and heart-felt. It emerged into faith. With longing heart he listened to the Word of the Lord. As he listened he was drawn. His heart was more fully opened. He believed.

Faith came by hearing, and hearing by the Word of God. It was a peculiar, and in some respects an extraordinary conversion. It was sudden and strongly marked. There was something of a miraculous agency in it. It was in part hastened by an earthquake. It will not do to take it for a general model. Those who want to be converted just as the jailor was, must needs have an earthquake accompaniment. Those who wish to be converted exactly as Paul was, must have a flash of blinding light from the sky, an audible voice, and a visible appearance of Jesus. These are extraordinary and miraculous features. They were only accompaniments. They did not carry converting power. That was carried in both cases, as it is in every case, by the living Word of God.

The jailor's also was an unusual case. He was an uncultured man. The animal naturally predominated over the intellectual. He would be influenced more strongly by feeling than by judgment, and this would have a tendency to make the change more or less violent in its manifestations. Again, the contrast between his former life and the new life would be much greater than in the case of Lydia. This also would tend to make his a strongly marked conversion.

There are sudden and strongly marked conversions still. But it will not do to make them the rule. They ought to be exceptions in the Church. It is better to grow up like Timothy than to be converted like Paul. It is far better to be filled with the Holy Ghost from the womb than to be converted like the jailor. Inside of the Church the Samuels and Jeremiahs and Johns and Timothys ought to be the rule, and the Sauls and jailors the exception. And if the Church had not drifted away from the old scriptural doctrine of baptismal

Grace and a baptismal covenant, such would still be the case. May the Lord help us to "*stand in the ways and see, and ask for the old paths, where is the good way, and walk therein.*"

We can only refer briefly to the *fruits* of the jailor's conversion:

We notice *first*, that here, as in Lydia's case, he was baptized *and all his*. It was another household baptism. The conversion of the head of the house brought the religion of Christ into the family. This is a blessed fruit of a true conversion. Let the heart of father or mother be changed, and the home will be changed. We know of a young man who said with bitterness, "Yes, my father can pray at prayer-meeting, but I never heard him pray at home." We doubted that father's religion. "*Let them learn first to show piety at home.*" When Zaccheus was converted, salvation came to his *house*. So to the jailor's.

A *second fruit*. He *rejoiced, believing with his whole house*. Faith brings joy into the heart and into the home. There is no joy like the Christian's joy. It banishes long faces, and heavy hearts, and complaining lips. It enables Paul and Silas to sing with glad hearts, though their backs are swollen and torn, and their feet are fast in the stocks. It brings a new joy into the heart of the formerly rough jailor, and his home becomes radiant with gladness. True, abiding joy is a fruit of true conversion.

Again: That formerly cruel man became merciful. He took those prisoners that same hour of the night *and washed their stripes.* Surely he had never done this before!

He had screwed the ankles of these men into the cruel stocks, and left them in their pain and anguish, a few hours ago. Now he gently, with his own hands, bathes the cuts and bruises, and allays their burning. What a change was here! He had obtained mercy, and he willingly exercises mercy.

The spirit of Christ is a spirit of mercy and good-will. It feeds the hungry and clothes the naked, and ministers to the sick and imprisoned. It does it in Jesus' name and for Jesus' sake. The world knew nothing of mercy to unfortunates and prisoners till it learned to know Christ. The exercise of mercy, pure and disinterested, is a fruit of conversion.

And *finally*, he showed *hospitality*. He brought the prisoners *into his house and set meat before them.* Think of a Roman jailor spreading his own table in the night, and inviting his prisoners to sit down and partake of his meat! Surely such a thing had never been heard of before. He had left those two prisoners in the evening in their agony and fever without even a drink of water. Now he spreads a table for them in his own house. Here was a change. The change of heart made the change of life. His conversion made him hospitable and liberal. It opened not only his heart but his home, his hand and his store. A blessed fruit of conversion.

Reader, are you converted? The question is not when, or where, or how; but are you *now* in a converted state? Have you now in your heart the elements of the new life? Do you hate, flee from, and mourn over sin? Do you constantly turn to the Lord Jesus Christ as your only Saviour and Redeemer? Do you *believe?* Do you *rejoice* believing? Does your religion show itself in your *home* life? Are you merciful? Are you liberal and hospitable? *"Examine yourself, whether you be in the faith: prove your own self."*

SERMON XVI.

A SPURIOUS CONVERSION.

Acts. viii. 9–14, and 18–25.

Acts viii. *9-14, and 18-25.* But there was a certain man called Simon, which beforetime in the same city used sorcery and bewitched the people of Samaria, giving out that himself was some great one:

To whom they all gave heed, from the least to the greatest, saying, This man is the great power of God.

And to him they had regard, because that of long time he had bewitched them with sorceries.

But when they believed Philip preaching the things concerning the kingdom of God, and the name of Jesus Christ, they were baptized, both men and women.

Then Simon himself believed also: and when he was baptized, he continued with Philip, and wondered; beholding the miracles and signs which were done. . . . . . .

And when Simon saw that through laying on of the apostles' hands the Holy Ghost was given, he offered them money, saying, Give me also this power, that on whomsoever I lay hands he may receive the Holy Ghost.

But Peter said unto him, Thy money perish with thee, because thou hast thought that the gift of God may be purchased with money.

Thou hast neither part nor lot in this matter. For thy heart is not right in the sight of God.

Repent therefore of this thy wickedness, and pray God, if perhaps the thought of thine heart may be forgiven thee.

For I perceive that thou art in the gall of bitterness, and in the bond of iniquity.

Then answered Simon, and said, Pray ye to the Lord for me, that none of these things which ye have spoken come upon me.

SERMON XVI.

AFTER the martyrdom of Stephen, the persecution raged fiercely against the young Church. That Church was now receiving its first baptism of blood. The blood of the martyr Stephen proved a prolific seed of the Church. The disciples, with the exception of the twelve Apostles, one of whom soon became a martyr also, *were scattered abroad throughout the regions of Judea and Samaria.* They went everywhere, *preaching the Word.* Philip went down to the city of Samaria, *and preached Christ unto them.* His success was wonderful. *The people with one accord gave heed unto those things which Philip spoke, hearing and seeing the miracles which he did.* Philip gathered in a great harvest, *and there was great joy in that city.*

But even there the enemy *sowed tares among the wheat,* and the Gospel net gathered in of fishes *both bad and good.* Simon the sorcerer had for a long time practiced the black art of sorcery among those rude and ignorant people. Man, even in the darkness of heathenism, feels that he is related to a higher world. He must believe something. He believes in and fears the unseen powers of an unseen world. This intuitive faith in the unseen, has always been utilized by imposters. They delude the ignorant and superstitious either by mere pretensions and juggleries, or receive aid in their sorceries from the *father of lies*, who is *the prince of the powers of the air, and worketh hitherto in the children of disobedience.*

Simon was one of these practitioners of the black art. He gave out that *himself was some great one.* He taught or encouraged the people to regard him as a sort of an incarnation, as *the great power of God.*

But when Philip came, preaching Christ and the things pertaining to the kingdom of God, Simon's former followers resorted to the evangelist, heard him gladly, and believed the Gospel which he preached. Simon, forsaken of his admirers, also came and heard the Word and saw the miracles that were wrought in the name of Jesus. He was astonished and professed conversion. The sequel shows that his was *a spurious conversion.* The account of it was no doubt written for our warning. We do well therefore to learn and take to heart its lessons.

We notice *first* his profession. He came and

listened to the preaching of Philip. He heard the plain and earnest Gospel message concerning Christ and His kingdom. Wherever this pure old Gospel is preached there is a wonderful charm and effectiveness about it. Simon no doubt felt himself drawn by its mysterious influence. That influence would make itself even more felt by winning a multitude of converts. So it is still. That old Gospel has not lost its power. It still interests and influences and moves the children of men. Even those who come to its preaching at first from curiosity are soon made to feel its mysterious movings. Philip accompanied the preaching of Christ with miracles wrought in His name. This astonished Simon still more. Who was this Christ, in whose name such mighty deeds could be done? Simon was persuaded that this Christ must be some great One. He was ready to believe in Him as a being possessing miraculous power. He professed to believe all that Philip said. He admitted that it must be historically true. He believed what was said about Christ, in the same sense in which he might have believed some orator setting forth the wonderful achievements of Alexander the Great or Julius Cæsar. It was an intellectual credence, a historic assent. Only this, and nothing more.

So it ever has been and so it is with multitudes of hearers still. They admit the truth of the Bible. They accept its facts and teachings just as they accept the contents of a biography of George Washington or Abraham Lincoln. They yield it a historic credence, and nothing more.

Simon went a step further. He not only gave credence to what he heard about Christ, but he publicly confessed his belief. We know from the record of the Acts that no adult was permitted to be baptized without making a profession of faith. Only on making such a profession were converts baptized and received into the communicant membership of the Church. Simon offered himself for baptism. He was accepted, and became a full member of the young Church at Samaria.

Philip was not omniscient. He could not see the heart. He could only hear the profession. On that he baptized Simon and admitted him into the congregation.

The apostles had likewise admitted Ananias and Sapphira into the congregation at Jerusalem. Now if inspired apostles and evangelists were thus imposed on by the insincere, why should it be thought a strange thing that such is still the case? The Church does not want it so. She does not encourage hypocrisy. If she did, then it would be fair to lay the blame on her. But as long as she faithfully protests against all insincerity and hypocrisy, as long as she earnestly warns against all sin, and shows the judgment of God against all such conduct, her skirts are clear, and it is the grossest injustice to hold these things up as a reproach on her fair name.

Wherever there is a pastor and congregation who encourage or even connive at a false profession, let *them* be held responsible.

We notice *secondly* the serious defects in Simon's case.

From the whole account it is clear that his heart remained in the world and still clung to the treasures of earth.

It is expected of every one who desires to become a follower of Christ, that he be willing to *deny himself and take up his cross* and follow Him. He who truly comes to Christ, in that very act renounces, gives up and sacrifices his former self-pleasing. His coming implies that instead of saying as theretofore, "What do *I* feel like doing?" he will henceforth say, "Lord, what wilt *thou* have me to do?"

Simon's idea was the very opposite of this.

When he saw Philip working miracles he longed to have this power also. When Peter and John came, and by the laying on of their hands imparted the gift to work miracles to certain persons, Simon wanted this apostolic power also.

Give me also this power, that on whomsoever I lay hands, he may receive the Holy Ghost. This was his request, and for the granting of it he was willing to pay.

Why did he want this power? Evidently that he might use it as he used his sorceries in former times. The people had paid him liberally for his deeds of magic. Here was something that transcended all his pretended powers. If he could acquire this feat, what a name it would give him! How he would then astound the multitudes far beyond those former days! And what money it would bring in! Everybody would be willing to pay for such an endowment from his hands! It would prove a bonanza, and make him a rich and renowned man! Yes, Simon had come into the Church, and now he wanted to make his Church membership *pay*.

It is a humiliating fact that Simon has had multitudes of followers. There are many who still come into the Church for worldly advantage.

Persons come into a new community. They visit and investigate the different churches in the place. For what purpose? Is it to find out where the Word of God is preached in its greatest purity, and where the sacraments are administered in accordance with the Word? This should be the motive. But, alas! these people are not looking for a spiritual home. They are not seeking truth. They are not in search of nourishment for the spiritual man. They are after *earthly gain*. They want to find out where the best society people go. They want social standing and advantage for themselves or their families. Where they find fashion, and tone, and popularity, there they will worship—popular favor!

Or, they are ambitious. They want to rise in the world. They desire a name and a fame. They would like to have a political office. Perhaps they can get it through the Church! In which church can they win the most influence, and gain the most votes? That shall be their church. There they will make profession—of a lie!

Or, they have an eye to business. They want customers for their wares. Which church will furnish the most? The writer knows of a commercial firm of four brothers: each one belongs to the leading church of a different denomination. Rumor says the object is to draw trade from all the denominations. Such persons are often quite liberal. They ostentatiously give large sums of money, because they believe it a good investment. They are the followers of Simon Magus. Godliness is gain with them. They are in the Church to bow down to mammon!

Now all such persons *have a name to live, while they are dead. They have a form of godliness, but know nothing of its power.* They may have witnessed a good confession before many witnesses. They may have used the sacraments and heard the Word. But they are unconverted Church members.

Such was Simon. Peter tells him that he is still *in the gall of bitterness.* His heart was still so full of sin, unrepented of and unforgiven, that it was like the overflowing of bitter gall.

He is still *in the bond of iniquity.* Iniquity fetters him like a bond. His spirit is bound with it as with a chain. He has the old deceitful and stony heart. It has not been softened by contrition. It has not been purified through faith. Even that semblance of repentance which he shows after Peter's scathing rebuke and denunciation, bears the mark of spuriousness on its face. He cries out cravenly: *"Pray ye to the Lord for me, that none of these things which ye have spoken come upon me."* Peter had exhorted him to pray. He says: *"Pray ye for me."* Ah yes, it is easy to ask for the prayers of the Church—any one can do that. It is no sure evidence of the workings of Grace. Peter had urged him to pray for *forgiveness.* He begs them to pray for removal of *punishment.* And who does not want punishment to be turned aside? Who does not desire immunity from suffering? It requires no Grace in the heart to want to be kept out of hell. Peter had assured him that *his heart was not right in the sight of God.* He makes no mention of a desire of a change of heart, but only that he may be safe against impending calamity. We can find neither penitence, nor faith, nor prayer in his response. It is only an abject cry of fear.

And oh, how sad is the fate which Peter pronounces upon this spurious convert! It is the fate of every Church member who is living in an unconverted state. *Thou hast neither part nor lot in this matter.*

Thou didst desire the miraculous and extraordinary gifts of the Spirit. Thou lackest even His ordinary influences. Thou hast not even permitted that Spirit to come through Word or sacrament to regenerate thy heart.

Thou knowest not even His renewing and sanctifying operations. Thou hast no part or lot at all in the Holy Ghost. Thou art an utter stranger to His life-giving and saving efficacy. Thou hast neither part nor lot in the forgiveness of sins, neither part nor lot in the kingdom of God. No part in Christ. No part in His purchased Redemption. No place in heaven. Ah, Simon, Simon! Thou mayest have many other things. But what shall it profit? Will thy other possessions help thee in the hour and article of death? Can they shield and save thee in the day of judgment?

Reader, have you a part and a lot in the redemption that is in Christ Jesus? Your name may be on the Church-roll. But is it in the Book of Life? You may regularly hear and read the Word. But is it to you *a savor of life unto life?* If not, it is *a savor of death unto death.* You go regularly to the Lord's table. But do you find that *Christ's flesh is meat indeed, and that His blood is drink indeed?* Or do you come unprepared, with impenitent and unbelieving heart, and thus *eat and drink judgment to yourself?* Have you a real, conscious, living and blessed part and lot in Christ?

SERMON XVII.

ALMOST CONVERTED.

ACTS xxiv. 24, 25.

Acts xxiv. *24, 25.* And after certain days, when Felix came with his wife Drusilla, which was a Jewess, he sent for Paul, and heard him concerning the faith in Christ.

And as he reasoned of righteousness, temperance, and judgment to come, Felix trembled and answered, Go thy way for this time; when I have a convenient season, I will call for thee.

SERMON XVII.

The Apostle Paul had been down to the city of Jerusalem. He had carried down money for the poor saints in that city, collected from the churches in Macedonia. It was the time of the Feast of Pentecost. Paul always kept these old festivals in their new spirit and significance. While worshipping in the temple he had been recognized by certain Asiatic Jews. These were carnally minded fellows, who had heard Paul preach in their own home, and had taken umbrage at his doctrine, and at him for preaching it. They became deeply enraged to see one who in their eyes was such an arch-heretic in the temple during the feast of Pentecost. They, therefore, "*stirred up all the people and laid hands on him, crying out: Men of Israel, help! This is the man that teacheth all men everywhere against the people, and the law, and this place: and further brought Greeks also into the temple, and hath polluted this holy place.*"

Paul was in imminent danger of being torn in pieces by the mob, and was only rescued by the quick and energetic interference of the captain of the guard of Roman soldiers stationed near the temple. The captain guarded him and permitted him to speak for himself from the steps of the castle. Paul made a straightforward defence of himself and his faith. The people heard him until he declared that he was sent by the Lord to preach unto the Gentiles. At this word the violence of the mob broke out afresh, and apparently to appease them, the captain ordered Paul to be scourged. From this indignity and torture Paul saved himself by declaring himself a Roman citizen. The captain now insisted that Paul should have a fair trial before the Sanhedrin, the highest court of the Jews. Here again Paul pleaded his own cause. The court broke up in a tumult, and the captain, *"fearing lest Paul should have been pulled in pieces of them, commanded the soldiers to go down and to take him by force from among them, and to bring him into the castle."*

And so Paul again escaped the lawless violence of his own countrymen. Chagrined because he had again escaped them, *"certain of the Jews banded themselves together, and bound themselves under a curse, saying, that they would neither eat nor drink till they had killed Paul."* But God was taking care of His servant. The conspiracy was reported to the captain. He at once arranged to transport Paul secretly and under a strong military escort to Cesarea, that he might have a fair trial before Felix, the Governor.

This Felix had been procurator of Judea for about six years. Historians inform us that he had been a slave, but had obtained his freedom, had fought with distinction in the Roman army, and through the influence of his brother Pallas, who was quite a favorite at the court of the Emperor Claudius, had been appointed Governor of Judea. He had ruled the province in a mean, cruel, and profligate manner. He had crucified hundreds of turbulent Jews and false Messiahs. He had bribed certain assassins to murder the High Priest Jonathan. Tacitus tells us in one sentence, that "by every form of cruelty and lust, he wielded the power of a king in the spirit of a slave." We are further told that he was the husband of three wives. Drusilla, whom we meet as his wife on this occasion, he had enticed away from her lawful husband, Azizus, king of Emesa. He was therefore living in open adultery with this Jewish mistress.

Before this Felix, Paul had had a hearing. It seems that the dignified, manly and straightforward course of Paul, had, from the very beginning, made a favorable impression on the Governor. But, to please the Jews, Paul was kept a prisoner, though given as much liberty as possible for one in custody. He was probably chained to a Roman soldier, and with him was allowed to be more or less at large.

Felix had probably told Drusilla about this unusual, interesting, and eloquent prisoner. She, being a Jewess, and knowing something of the faith of her fathers, also of that *new way which they called heresy*, desired to see and hear this prisoner preacher of Christ. To gratify her, Paul was sent for and given the privilege of declaring to this royal and profligate couple *the faith in Christ*. Paul, like his Lord, was no respecter of persons. He always preached the truth, and declared the whole counsel of God, regardless of the fear or favor of man. What a temptation to flatter! Paul knew that Felix by a nod of his head could set him free, and by a word could hand him over to death. But he was not turned aside from a straightforward course. His discourse is not given. We are simply told that Felix sent for him, *and heard him concerning the faith in Christ.* No doubt Paul told him fully and plainly of that *faith*. And then, as an application of the doctrine, as an exhortation, growing out of and built on the preceding instruction concerning the faith, Paul reasoned of *righteousness, temperance, and judgment to come.*

The result of this sermon was that Felix was

ALMOST CONVERTED.

And this shall be the subject of the present discourse. To be almost converted is certainly to be in a very serious and critical state. It is to be near the kingdom of God, and yet not necessarily certain of a place in that kingdom.

We inquire then, *first* of all, what does it mean to be almost converted?

It means, in the first place, that *the mind has been enlightened* in spiritual things. So it was with Felix. We read that he *had a more perfect knowledge*—or understanding—*of that way*, i. e., the *way that they called heresy*, or the doctrines preached by Paul. During the six years that he had ruled among the Jews he had learned something of their faith. He would learn still more from his Jewish wife Drusilla. Of the *new* way or Christianity, he must also have known something. It was now nearly thirty years since the resurrection of Jesus, the coming of the Spirit, and the first preaching of the apostles. The first Gentile converts had been made eighteen years ago among the troops of that very city of Cesarea. This *new way* was therefore well known. It was *everywhere spoken against*, and therefore everywhere spoken about. So Felix must have understood something about it even before Paul came. And now Paul had given that clear account and made that masterly defense in the presence of his Jewish accusers and of Felix. A second time Felix had sent for Paul that he might hear further for himself and Drusilla, *concerning the faith in Christ.*

His mind, therefore, was enlightened. He knew something about Christ and His redemption, and himself as a sinner, needing that redemption. And this is a vitally important step towards conversion. When that scribe came to Jesus and questioned Him about the law, *and when Jesus saw that he answered discreetly, He said unto him, Thou art not far from the kingdom of God.* His mind was enlightened, and *therefore* he was near the kingdom, or almost converted.

When Paul was pleading before Agrippa, he appealed to Agrippa as one *expert in all questions and customs which are among the Jews.* And again, "*King Agrippa, believest thou the prophets? I know that thou believest.*" The king's mind was enlightened, and *therefore* he was *almost persuaded* to be a Christian. And so it always is. When the mind is enlightened by the Word of God; when the sinner is made to understand what he is, what he needs, where and how to get what he needs, then there is an important step taken towards conversion. But this divine illumination is not in itself conversion.

A second step is when the *conscience is aroused.* In his application of the doctrine of Christ, Paul *reasoned* of *righteousness*, or uprightness, *temperance*, or chastity, and *judgment to come.*

Before that unrighteous ruler whose reign was stained with rapine and blood, Paul reasoned of *righteousness*, right-doing, uprightness, moral character. And so forcibly did he reason, so directly did he appeal to the conscience of his hearer, that that conscience was aroused from its torpor. And Felix felt, without Paul telling him: *"thou art the man*, thou art verily guilty of gross and criminal unrighteousness." Unless thou seek to the righteousness of this Christ now set before thee, thou art justly condemned.

Paul reasoned of *temperance.* The word in the original means continence or chastity. Before this libidinous queen and her lustful paramour, Paul reasoned of the duty and beauty of a chaste life. Without Paul's pointing out their shameful breaches of morality, they quailed under his words, and conscience held before them their guilt.

And finally Paul reasoned of a *judgment to come.* Awful time! When every evil thought, every idle word, and every sinful deed, shall be brought to light and impartially judged. No wonder that the guilty and now fully awakened conscience of Felix spoke in thunder tones, and *Felix trembled.* Self-condemned and self-convicted, he sat pale with excitement. Surely the scales were turned. The prisoner preacher had become the judge. The Governor was the defendant. Alarmed and stricken, he acknowledged to himself that he was guilty. When the conscience of the sinner is thus stirred and alarmed, then another important step is taken towards conversion.

But more than this. We believe that *the heart* of the Governor *was touched* also. We believe that as he saw and felt his own guilt and misery, he had some longings after deliverance and a better life. If his heart had not been touched and drawn, we believe he would have dismissed the Apostle in anger. But he did not. He simply intimated that he could bear no more now. But he wanted to hear more at another time. He was so deeply impressed that he wanted to think it all over. He hoped at some other time to learn more and become fully satisfied.

Here was a third important step. The heart was moved and drawn. And when the heart is thus reached and impressed, when there go up from it unuttered yearnings after deliverance and righteousness, then surely *Jesus of Nazareth is passing by*. The sinner is *almost* converted. Surely, Felix was in a hopeful way. The mind was enlightened. The conscience was aroused. The heart was moved. What lacked he yet? One other faculty must be reached and changed. The *will* must give its assent. If it does, Felix will be *entirely* converted.

Before we look, however, at the obstacles that often prevent an entire conversion, we inquire *secondly* into the causes that bring the sinner thus almost into the kingdom.

The prime and original cause of all such experiences is always *the Holy Spirit*. He comes first to the sinner. He operates through the written and sacramental Word. As we have elsewhere shown, the Word is His organ and instrument. Through it He enlightens, convicts and draws. Through the Word He operated on Felix. He convinced him of his own sin, of his need of another's righteousness, and of a fearful looking for of judgment for all who are not clothed in the righteousness of the Substitute. And wherever a sinner is thus enlightened, convinced, and drawn, it is always a work of the Spirit of God. It is Divine Grace reaching down to save him. And no one was ever thus reached and drawn towards the kingdom of God except by the Spirit through the Word.

True, God sometimes uses other influences as helps to reach the sinner. He sends upon him grievous affliction. He gives him over to bitter losses and disappointments. He lays upon him His chastening hand. Some people imagine that such afflicting and correcting dispensations convert the sinner. But this is a mistake. Affliction and correction carry no Divine Grace. They have no renewing or sanctifying power. They are only intended to drive the sinner to the Word and to make him attentive thereto. They are like the shepherd's crook. It cannot satisfy the hunger or thirst of the sheep, but he uses it to drive them to the green pastures and beside the still waters. The chastenings of the Lord are not His vehicles of Grace, but they drive to Word and Sacrament which are. In so far, and in so far only, are they helps in drawing the sinner towards the kingdom.

Again, when there is *a general interest* in the things pertaining to the kingdom of God. When others are coming to Christ. When friends, acquaintances and neighbors are finding Him, this also has a tendency to make the sinner think, to draw his attention to the neglected Word, to take him where that Word is preached. In the days of Felix there was a deep interest in these questions concerning the faith of Christ. Not only in Jerusalem, but in every city where the apostles had preached, no small stir was made about this new way. At Cesarea, Cornelius and his household had long since embraced the new faith. Philip, the evangelist, with his four daughters who had the gift of prophecy, lived there. Other disciples also were there. There must have been a congregation, and regular services. All this may also have had an influence on Felix and his Jewish wife Drusilla, and induced them to send for Paul to hear more of this faith in Christ. And thus did Felix come to be almost converted. And thus are sinners still brought near to the kingdom.

But not all who are almost converted become entirely converted. They refuse to take the decisive step. They decline to make the final surrender. While the intellect, the conscience and the heart have all become interested, the will refuses, resists and rebels. And as long as the will does not entirely surrender, no matter what the knowledge, the conviction and the feelings may be, there is no real conversion. The final decision rests with the will. Its yielding is the decisive step in conversion.

True, it is already influenced from above. When the Holy Spirit has reached the understanding, the conscience and the feelings of the heart, the will is more or less influenced. Divine Grace is at work upon it. With the help of that Grace, it can surrender, turn to Christ and accept the proffered salvation.

But while it can do this only in the strength given by the Holy Ghost, for *no man can say that Jesus is the Christ, but by the Holy Ghost*, it can also, without any outside assistance whatever, resist and refuse. While God, therefore, always comes first to man, and while man can do nothing except with the help that God gives, yet the final determination rests with man, and on himself alone is the responsibility if he is not saved.

We notice, therefore, *thirdly*, some of the obstacles that keep men who are almost converted from being entirely converted, or some of the influences that determine the will in deciding against Christ.

What are some of the dreadful hindrances that hold back persons who are not far from the kingdom of God, and finally shut them out from that kingdom?

Very often people are brought to the very door of the kingdom, divine Grace has done a saving work in them, they are almost and all but converted, and yet they are not saved. They are kept out *by holding on to one sin*. They have one evil practice. They cherish it openly or secretly. They are in love with it. They feel, when reached, as described above, that it is dragging them down to hell. They may even cry out in anguish on account of the fearful hold it has on them. It has wound its frightful coils so tightly about their life. It seems burnt into the very fibre of their being. They are ready to cry out in agony, "*Oh, wretched man that I am, who shall deliver me from the body of this death?*" They rattle the chains of their slavery, and anon they clutch and kiss them as if they were cords that were drawing them to heaven. The question is forced upon them, Shall I give up entirely and forever this sin? The answer is, I cannot, *because I will not*. Angels' hands are reaching down to release them. They ask, Shall I yield? Shall I give up this sin? No; I will not. And with a determined effort they beat back the hand that is reaching down to save them. They were almost in the kingdom. They might have entered in. But that one sin, wilfully held on to, stands like an evil spirit between them and the kingdom, and shuts its gates against them.

Oh, the power of one cherished and therefore unforgiven sin! It has kept thousands out of heaven when they were almost in. Felix was almost converted, but he would not give up his adultery with Drusilla. Herod heard the Word of God gladly from the Baptist's lips, and was drawn towards the kingdom, but he would not restore his brother Philip's wife. Judas, no doubt, had his better moments and his serious impressions, and felt himself drawn to the blessed Jesus. But he loved money, and was unwilling to give up that love. Ananias and Sapphira were drawn by the apostles' preaching, and wanted a place in the infant Church. But wanted to serve God and mammon, and lied to the Holy Ghost. That one sin kept them out of the church invisible.

And is it not so still? Many even in the Church are cherishing some pet sin. They know it is standing between them and their God. They sometimes weep over it, and tremble on account of it. But they will not give it up. Often almost converted, they die unconverted and are lost. Others are kept out of the Church, though often on the point of going in and giving themselves to Christ, because unwilling to give up one particular sin.

Again, it may be *bad company* that holds such persons back. Some godless person has obtained a fatal influence over them. It may be more than one person. They are almost persuaded to be Christians. They are on the point of surrendering. Suddenly the thought comes, What would that companion say? I would have to cut his acquaintance and give up his friendship, unless I could get him to go with me. No, I dread his displeasure. I am afraid of his ridicule. I could never face him again. I ought to be a Christian. I wish I were a Christian. But, for the sake of that person *I'll not yield*. And thus these persons are under the fatal charm of some evil companion, and rather than break with that companion, they deliberately turn their backs on their Redeemer, and drive away the good Spirit who was striving to save them. The thought of his associates may have had something to do with holding Felix back. It may also have kept him out of the kingdom of whom Jesus said, "Thou art not far from the kingdom." It has doubtless kept out thousands, and is doing so to-day.

Others again are almost converted, but when it comes to the final decision they *dread the sacrifices* they will have to make. They would like to have the crown of life, but are unwilling to *strive* for it. They love the world, its pleasures, its honors, or its riches, so much that they dread giving up these pursuits. They shrink from the self-denial and cross-bearing which Jesus imposes. They dread the burdens of discipleship. They forget that the burdens which Jesus imposes are like the weights of a clock, the old man's staff, or the burdens of a bird's wing. Balaam wanted to *die the death of the righteous*, but was not willing to give up *the wages of unrighteousness.* The rich youth wanted eternal life, but he was unwilling to tear his heart from the love of his possessions. Demas was a disciple and even a fellow-helper with the apostles, but he forsook them, *having loved this present world.* And so thousands forfeit eternal life and the riches of heaven, because they dread giving up something that affords momentary gratification to the flesh. Almost converted sometimes, they are never entirely converted, because they fear the burdens, which are really no burdens to the true disciple.

And finally, others are kept out of the kingdom because they *put off* their entrance to a more convenient season. Oh, what uncounted numbers are to-day in hell, who were more than once almost converted. They were not entirely converted because they said to the Spirit, "*Go thy way for this time; when I have a convenient season I will call for thee.*" Thus did Felix grieve away the good Spirit. Many seasons came, for he sent for Paul often and communed or conversed with him.

But he had deliberately shaken off serious impressions, resisted the Spirit who was trying to save, stifled conviction, hardened his own heart, and was now less and less open to good impressions. He became harder and harder. He wanted an unlawful bribe from Paul. He became more and more wicked, and came to a miserable end.

It is indeed an awful thing to trifle with conviction. It is a serious thing to be almost converted, and then deliberately to turn back to the world. In most cases it means to deliberately start towards hell.

How sad the results of being almost converted, and yet not entirely! With Felix we have seen that the refusal was fatal.

Every such opportunity unimproved leaves the sinner harder in heart and harder to reach. It gives him an impetus downward.

And when finally such an one is lost, must it not be much harder to bear than if he had never been touched by divine Grace? How hard for the seafarer, after coming safely through the tempests and dangers of a long sea voyage, to be wrecked and drowned with the shore-lights in sight. And what must it be to have been so near heaven. To have almost looked inside. To have almost heard the rustle of angel wings and the music of angel harps—and then to find himself in hell. Almost—*but lost.*

> "Almost persuaded" now to believe;
> "Almost persuaded" Christ to receive;
> Seems now some soul to say,
> "Go, Spirit, go Thy way,
> Some more convenient day
>   On Thee I'll call."

> "Almost persuaded," Come, come to-day;
> "Almost persuaded," Turn not away;

ALMOST CONVERTED.

Jesus invites you here,
Angels are lingering near,
Prayers rise from hearts so dear:
  O wanderer, come.

"Almost persuaded," harvest is past!
"Almost persuaded," doom comes at last!
"Almost" cannot avail;
"Almost" is but to fail!
Sad, sad, that bitter wail—
  " Almost—*but lost!*"

www.ingramcontent.com/pod-product-compliance
Lightning Source LLC
Chambersburg PA
CBHW032117230426
43672CB00009B/1767